This essay is dedicated to

Caroline Lai Hung Blair

麗 虹

and to her much abused generation

Look Up:

*Effective Collective Action to Stop the Slow Motion
Intergenerational Genocide of Global Warming*

Russell Blair

Other Essays By Russell Blair

Latin America

Americano: Una lengua común para la Comunidad de Estados Latinoamericanos y Caribeños (2010)
Americano: Mobilizing Generation Todos Juntos (2020)

Africa

Afrançais: Le français en tant que langue africaine (2012)

Europe

European: An Identity Language for the EU (2012)
Speaking for Europe: Unity, Legitimacy and Global Leadership (2013)
Governing Diversity (2016)
How Brexit Can Save the EU (2017)
Taalvrede: De kritieke kwestie bij de federale verkiezingen van 2019 (2018)
Pax linguistique: La question cruciale lors des élections fédérales de 2019 (2018)
Language Peace in Belgium and the European Union (2018)
Belgische Eenheid: De zevende staatshervorming (2019)
Unité Belge: La septième réforme de l'État (2019)
Speaking For Europe's Future (2019)

The Commonwealth

The Post Brexit Commonwealth (2017)
The Commonwealth: Multilingual Congruence, Kissinger's Challenge & Kant's Perpetual Peace (2018)
This essay was the first to use the term complementary bilingualism.

India

Modi's Moment, India's Future (2019)

Global Language Rationalization

Balancing Eurasia: The Foundation for Global Collective Action (2020)
UN 2021: Regional Coherence, Global Community and Three Things to Do Right Now (2021)
This essay was the first to use the term 2MT complementary bilingualism.
Our Bilingual Future: A Global Community of Communication (2021)

Contents

"Communication is what makes us human; and if history were written with this simple notion in mind, networks of communication would become the center of attention, and a more satisfactory history of the world (and of all the innumerable subordinate groupings of human-kind) might emerge." (*Emphasis added*)

William H. McNeill, foreword to *The World System: Five Hundred Years or Five Thousand?* (1992)

Introduction:

A Global Community of Common Fate

1) We are a global community - a community of common fate. Our global community was created by our common and existential problems (global warming, nuclear proliferation, global pandemics, global poverty and immiseration, etc.). Our choice is between being a functional community or a dysfunctional community.

2) Global problems require a collective and synchronized response; otherwise, the free rider problem will prevent their solution. Our current capacity for collective action is clearly inadequate.

3) A collective and synchronized response requires multi-state governance, but not a global government. Global governance can only succeed under the right conditions.

4) Global governance requires legitimacy, if it is to be effective and stable. This essay is about establishing the necessary legitimacy.

5) Governments can base their legitimacy on a variety of factors; ethnolinguistic solidarity and congruence, cultural solidarity and congruence,

religious solidarity and congruence - but global governance must be based on either process legitimacy (democracy) or coercion. Coercion is neither desirable nor possible.

6)   Democratic global governance, like a democratic nation-state government, requires congruence between a community of communication and the institutions of governance. Being outvoted by people with whom one cannot communicate is perceived as tyranny, not democracy.

7)   Because global elite bilingualism has failed, a language rationalization policy of complementary bilingualism is the essential first step in the global governance necessary for the resolution of global problems.

8)   Complementary bilingualism will have an immediate and powerful cohesive effect from the commitment to a defining and superordinate goal.

9)   The current world order is engaged in slow-motion intergenerational genocide. The generations at risk need a global identity. The identity function of a common language is the only way to accomplish this. We can coalesce around a policy of complementary bilingualism which will make us a global community of direct communication.

The Essay Dissected

The nation-state model chose hegemonic monolingualism for language rationalization (Chapter 3). That policy is not an option in the 21st Century. For post nation-state aggregations like the EU and the AU (Region-States) or in India, it is necessary to use a new type of language rationalization: complementary bilingualism (Chapter 5). It will also allow global language rationalization (Chapter 6). Complementary bilingualism does not require the conflict, coercion and bloodshed that occurred in the establishment of hegemonic monolingualism and it achieves the same congruence without sacrificing linguistic and cultural diversity.

Governments resist language rationalization because of the unexamined assumption that linguistic diversity and linguistic unity are irreconcilable. Complementary bilingualism resolves that tension, permitting congruence in multi-national and multi-state polities while preserving unlimited diversity. With complementary bilingualism we can even become a global community of communication without sacrificing any of our collective diversity. Becoming a global community is crucial to increasing our capacity for the collective action needed to resolve our global problems.

> "The simplest reason would tell each individual that he ought to extend his social instincts and sympathies to all the members of the same nation, though personally unknown to him. This point being once reached, there is only an artificial barrier to prevent his sympathies extending to all men of all nations and races."
>
> Charles Darwin, *The Descent of Man* (1871)

Human groups cooperate with those they perceive as "us" but not with those they perceive as "them." Through cultural evolution, humans have increased the potential size of "us." In this century, we need to create a global "us" in order to effectively respond to our global problems. The consequences of a failure to pick the low hanging fruit of linguistic unity will be less global cooperation, unnecessary conflict and unprecedented human suffering.

Our failure to realize our bilingual potential leaves us divided into thousands of linguistically divided communities. With tremendous and universal benefit, complementary bilingualism can *easily* be initiate at the multi-state, multi-national or global levels. The benefits from doing so will be multiple orders of magnitude greater than the effort required.

> "There can be little doubt that size itself can be a group-level adaptation. Larger societies tend to replace smaller societies *unless their larger size is offset by problems of coordination* and internal conflicts of interest." (Emphasis added.)
>
> David S. Wilson, *Darwin's Cathedral: Evolution, Religion and the Nature of Society* (2002)

Part I. The Current Global Order

The first part of the essay is composed of two chapters that explain the current dominance of three empire-states: the USA, China and Russia. Chapter 1 introduces necessary concepts and corrects several myths about the current global order. Chapter 2 discusses the history of empires in the 20th Century, focusing on the extinction of the *multilingual* empires, *revisionist* empires, *colonial* empires and one *ideological* empire. Only one type of empire survived – the empire-state – and three empire-states now monopolize international agency: USA, China and Russia.

> "… listening to people speak a language you can't understand is a strange and maddening experience. It can be more than that. It can be the origin of prejudice and hostility. If you are unable to talk to someone, it's hard to appreciate how much you have in common."
>
> David Shariatmadari, *Don't Believe a Word: The Surprising Truth About Language* (2020)

Part II. Congruence is Essential

The second part of the essay also has two chapters. The first of these chapters discusses the history of linguistic congruence in the nation-state model. Currently, linguistic congruence between a demos (citizens) and a polity (state) is limited to a subset of nation-states and all three three of the empire-states. Linguistic congruence is not even on the agendas of the inchoate region-states (EU and AU) and this omission has limited their success. It also needs to be on the agenda of the UN, to globalize and maximize our capacity for collective action.

The second of the two chapters in this part explains both the non-governmental and governmental benefits of bilingualism, with a focus on 2MT complementary bilingualism. This chapter sets the stage for the discussion of complementary bilingualism's ability to increase our capacity for collective action.

"... because of differences of language, all the similarity of their common human nature is of no avail to unite them in fellowship. So true is this that a man would be more cheerful with his dog for company than with a foreigner."

St. Augustine, *The City of God* (Circa 400 AD)

Part III. Increasing Our Capacity to Solve Global Problems

We are a global community. It is not a choice. It is a result of the global nature of the problems confronting us. This essay does not propose specific solutions to particular problems. The specific responses to global problems are best covered elsewhere, written by experts in each specific case. Our current problems will not be the last problems we face collectively. This essay is about creating the social infrastructure to increase our capacity to solve *any* global problem.

Successful global collective action *begins* with the creation of a global community of communication. That is the topic of the final chapter. Global communication is not a silver bullet, but it is a necessary condition for maximizing global collective action. Establishing this essential condition is the fastest way to improve global collective action. Fortunately, this first step is both simple and powerful.

Part I

The Current Global Order

"The new world order is an order of empires – empires like China, like India, like Russia, like the United States of America... Only together in a real European union, can we succeed and survive."

Guy Verhofstadt, Candidate for EU Commission President and Former Prime Minister of Belgium (May 2, 2019)

Chapter 1

Preliminary Matters

World order in the 21st century is dominated by what Guy Verhofstadt (above) correctly classifies as empires. I differ from Mr. Verhofstadt only in recognizing India as distinct from the other three. The others have linguistic congruence, using a language rationalization policy of hegemonic monolingualism. They are empire-states. India's lack of linguistic congruence makes it the least cohesive of the four. To reflect this difference, India is referred to as an inchoate empire-state.

Understanding the future prospects for global collective action begins with an understanding of the true nature of the current global order, which is almost universally misrepresented as a system of nation-states. Understanding the true nature of global order requires the use of several concepts that are absent or obscure in most discussions and the correction of six myths. Some of the concepts required the creation of neologisms that bring into focus phenomena whose existence is overlooked or, at least, under-appreciated.

"When I use a word," Humpty Dumpty said in a rather scornful tone, "it means just what I choose it to mean – neither more nor less."

Lewis Carroll, *Through the Looking Glass, and What Alice Found There* (1871)

1.1 Necessary Concepts

Like Humpty Dumpty, my use of words can be idiosyncratic. Hopefully, these definitions lower the risk of miscommunication. The idiosyncratic use of standard terms and the judicious creation of neologisms is useful, perhaps essential, for the reconsideration of conventional beliefs. Neologisms permit a focus on aspects that are hidden or ambiguous in standard usage. One neologisms, *complementary bilingualism*, is central to this essay.

Linguistic Concepts

(1) Plurilingualism (Individual) verses Multilingualism (Community). It is important to distinguish between plurilingualism and multilingualism. Plurilingualism refers to an individual's ability to use more than one language and move between them (code switching). Multilingualism is the community-level cohabitation of more than one language. For example, the European Union (EU) has a *community* policy of *aspirational trilingual plurilingualism* for its individual citizens. This plurilingual policy is abbreviated as MT + 2 (one mother tongue + two foreign languages). The EU's *institutional* policy is *elite multilingualism* (English, French and German). In contrast, as defined below, complementary bilingualism is a single policy for both a community's citizens (demos) and its institutions of governance (polity).

(2) Linguistic Congruence. Linguistic congruence is the alignment of a language community with the institutions of governance. Hegemonic monolingualism ensures linguistic congruence. Complementary bilingualism is an alternative way to establish congruence. It is the only way to achieve congruence in a linguistically diverse environment without a loss of diversity.

(3) Complementary Bilingualism. In linguistically diverse environments, complementary bilingualism adds a common second language to every individual's mother tongue. This creates congruence. The essence of complementary bilingualism is that it permits unlimited direct communication, the creation of a shared narrative, and a common identity in a linguistically diverse community and simultaneously maintains linguistic diversity. Complementary bilingualism can add either an indigenous

(internal) or an exogenous (external) language. The key to complementary bilingualism is early bilingual education in every child's family language and in a common language.

Starting in Part II, the term complementary bilingualism is sometimes specified as 2MT complementary bilingualism. 2MT stands for *two mother tongues*. As discussed in Section 4.3, children can learn two languages simultaneously and doing so is both cost effective and dual identity enhancing. For parents who are not comfortable with bilingualism at home, the very early introduction of the common language in elementary school will be sufficient. Young children have an amazing capacity for plurilingualism.

(4) Elite Bilingualism. An incomplete form of complementary bilingualism is elite bilingualism. An elite language can be a barrier to upward mobility by restricting elite status and its associated privileges. The identity function of the language has been co-opted by an elite minority. Instead of creating an inclusive identity, it creates elite closure. Elite bilingualism is common, at least initially, in post-colonial governance. It can be converted to full complementary bilingualism by providing adequate educational support for both multiple indigenous languages, in those places where each is predominant, and a common language.

(5) Language Rationalization. Language rationalization has historically been a matter of reducing linguistic diversity to establish congruence between a population (demos) and the institutions of governance (polity). This reflects the utility of hegemonic monolingualism for the nation-state model and the establishment of democracy. Language rationalization with a policy of complementary bilingualism achieves the same benefits without the conflict, coercion and bloodshed that was required for hegemonic monolingualism. Language rationalization now has two models. Only complementary bilingualism is plausible for use in the 21st Century.

There are four points of reference on my language rationalization continuum. The absence of rationalization, on the left end of the continuum, is *laissez faire* multilingualism for institutions and *laissez faire* plurilingualism for citizens. *Laissez faire* multilingualism doesn't necessarily occur in the absence of an official language. A *de facto* hegemonic language can emerge without being official. English in the USA is an example.

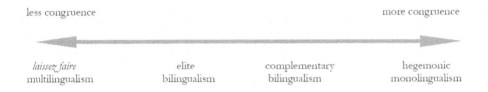

less congruence			more congruence
laissez faire multilingualism	elite bilingualism	complementary bilingualism	hegemonic monolingualism

Political Concepts

(6) <u>Nation-State</u>. In this essay, the term nation-state is used for countries with linguistic congruence, or which at least actively aspire to have linguistic congruence. The difference between my usage and the standard usage is clarified by considering Spain. Because it includes the Basque, Catalan, and Galician ethnolinguistic nations, Spain is sometimes referred to as a multinational state rather than a nation-state. This is a useful distinction in some contexts but is not relevant here. Because Castilian is hegemonic, Spain has linguistic congruence and is considered a nation-state. States that are coextensive with a single nation, like Japan and Iceland, are rare.

(7) <u>Empire-State</u>. An empire-state is a *very large, powerful* and *contiguous* polity that was created by the assimilation of at least one ethnolinguistic minority. An empire-state has the critical attribute of linguistic congruence. Because of this powerful combination, the three monolingual empire-states (USA, China, and Russia) currently monopolize international agency.

(8) <u>Region-State</u>. A region-state is the aggregation of nation-states into a regional polity with linguistic congruence. The term reflects their similarity to nation-states and empire-states. Currently, there are no region-states, but there are at least two inchoate region-states that lack linguistic congruence and are not yet actively seeking congruence. If they achieve linguistic congruence, the European Union (EU) and African Union (AU) will be able to create the political institutions necessary to be competitive with the empire-states. The need to be competitive motivates their current

attempts to evolve from diverse nation-states with individual sovereignty into region-states with international agency.

1.2 Six Myths Corrected

Due to the short duration of a human life and thus of personal experience, people accord current circumstances a sense of permanence and stability that is unwarranted. The human time scale must be supplemented by an appreciation for the long duration of both cultures and civilizations. A longer temporal perspective will correct at least six prevalent myths.

Myth #1: Nation-states are the basis for modern governance and global order.

Correction: Europe developed the monolingual nation-state model over hundreds of years of coercion and bloodshed. The European model was exported globally, primarily through colonialism and almost always with an elite language for administration. The global export of the European nation-state model, often imperfectly realized with elite bilingualism, caused the number of nation-states to increase and appear to be the basis of global order. However, this perspective overlooks the dominant empire-state model, which is represented by three *contiguous and monolingual empires*: China, Russia, and the USA (Chapter 2).

The *multilingual, revisionist* and *colonial* empires, along with one *ideological* empire, were destroyed in the 20th century. The result was new nation-states. The empire-states that survived and thrived are hiding in plain sight. Their hegemonic monolingualism leads people to misperceive them as examples of the nation-state model. A more productive view is to recognize them as empire-states. Empire-state status is an emergent property. At an imprecise and subjective point on the continuum of size, a further quantitative increase in size has qualitative consequences. Like beauty, it is hard to define but you know it when you see it.

Myth #2: Sovereignty confers international agency.

Correction: Closely related to the myth of nation-state preeminence is the myth of nation-state agency. Sovereignty is the *de jure* right, under international law, to choose internal policies. Agency is the *de facto* power to influence the terms of the available policy choices—both among polities and within those polities whose sovereignty is compromised by their size. International agency requires a polity with a combination of size (geographic, demographic, military, and economic) and the coherence of linguistic congruence. Currently, international agency is monopolized by the three empire-states.

Myth #3: Linguistic congruence between citizens (demos) and the institutions of governance (polity) requires monolingualism. French citizens speak French. German citizens speak German. There is a conflict in language rationalization between efficiency and the preservation of diversity.

Correction: Monolingual congruence prioritizes efficiency at the expense of diversity. Complementary bilingualism, because it uses two languages, can preserve diversity while providing an efficiency that is comparable to monolingualism. An unstructured policy (*laissez-faire*), whether individual plurilingualism or institutional multilingualism, does not guarantee congruence. Only complementary bilingualism has the ability to establish congruence while preserving linguistic and cultural diversity.

Myth #4: Nation-states are too different from each other for regional governance to successfully combine nation-states to the degree required for them to achieve international agency.

Correction: Nation-state and regional governance are not mutually exclusive. Governance can be thought of as the layering of appropriate competencies. A good metaphor is the famous Russian Matryoshka Dolls. Competencies are already layered within nation-states. It takes only a little imagination to extend the idea of layering *appropriate* competencies and assigning high politics to a region-state. Region-state high politics (defense and foreign relations) is the necessary minimum for them to achieve international agency.

> "If in the Middle Ages you had dared to predict the death of Latin as the language of education, people would have laughed in your face..."
> David Crystal, *English as a Global Language* (1997)

Myth #5: English has an insurmountable lead as the world's *lingua franca*.

Correction: To appreciate the potential for the displacement of *lingua franca* English, consider the recent experience of Russian as a *lingua franca*. When the USSR adopted perestroika (restructuring) and glasnost (openness) policies in 1985, Hungary began retraining 1,000 Russian language teachers to teach German. As reported in the Moscow Times on November 28, 2019, Russia's Education Ministry estimated that the number of students learning Russian as a second language had dropped by almost 50% since the end of the USSR, from 74.6 million to 38.2 million. Outside of the ex-USSR Republics, the number of students learning Russian fell from 20 million to 1 million. English *as a second language* is equally fragile.

Myth #6: Democratic governments cannot engage in language planning and policymaking, because citizens will not let them rationalize the community's language use.

Correction: Democracy *required* language rationalization. It was only because the nation-state model included language rationalization that democracy was possible. The nation-state model chose hegemonic monolingualism for language rationalization (Chapter 3). That policy is not an option in the 21st Century. However, for democracy to be established in post nation-state aggregations like the EU and the AU (Region-States) or in India, it is necessary to engage in a new type of language rationalization: complementary bilingualism (Chapter 5). The same rationalization policy will allow global language rationalization (Chapter 6). Complementary bilingualism is the necessary language rationalization policy for the 21st Century. It does not require the conflict, coercion and bloodshed that occurred with hegemonic monolingualism and it achieves the same benefits without sacrificing linguistic and cultural diversity.

"Without official recognition, the fate of the best system (of language rationalization) is precarious; with it, any scheme that is not totally unworkable would do well enough."

Albert Léon Guérard, *A Short History of the International Language Movement* (1921)

"No theory, no promises, no morality, no amount of good will, no religion will restrain power.... Only power restrains power."

James Burnham, *The Machiavellians: Defenders of Freedom* (1943)

Chapter 2

Great Power Rivalry: Empires and Empire-States

The term *empire* needs to be parsed in order to understand the changes in the world order that occurred during the 20th century. In the 19th century, the empire model included both monolingual and multilingual empires. Some empires were contiguous, like the Austro-Hungarian and Ottoman empires, others were not, like the British and French colonial empires. Three contiguous empires also had hegemonic monolingualism: USA, Russia and China. Their combination of linguistic congruence and contiguous size made them qualitatively different. They were empire-states.

> "Twentieth-century violence is unintelligible if it is not seen in its imperial context. For it was in large measure a consequence of the decline and fall of the large multiethnic empires that had dominated the world in 1900. What nearly all the principal combatants in the world wars had in common was that they either were empires or sought to become empires."
>
> Niall Ferguson, *The War of the World: Twentieth-Century Conflict and the Descent of the West* (2006)

2.1 The 20th Century's Empire Wars

During the 20th century, both the *multilingual* and the *colonial* empires were destroyed by the empire-states. The dominance of the three empire-states was the primary effect of 20th-century conflict. World Wars I and II are often seen as conflicts that overturned the empire model and universalized the nation-state model. In fact, the 20th century only demonstrated the weakness of the *colonial* and *multilingual* empires and the greater fitness of the empire-state model. Nation-states were allies of the dominant empire-states. Implicitly, if not explicitly, degrees of empire-state suzerainty were central to the global order.

The weakness of the *multilingual* empires first became evident in the second half of the 19th century. This was, not coincidentally, the golden age of the formation of European nation-states. During the 20th century, both the multilingual and colonial empires collapsed. Empires, though fewer in number, remained dominant. The empire model was refined into the empire-state model.

2.1.1 <u>World War I: *Multilingual* Empires Shattered</u>. World War I resulted in the destruction of two multilingual empires (the Austro-Hungarian and Ottoman empires) by the combined forces of two *colonial* empires (Great Britain and France) and two empire-states (USA and Russia).

Because Russia withdrew from the war after the overthrow of its tsar, its territorial objectives at the start of the war are not well-remembered. If Russia had stayed the course, history would have been dramatically different. The Russian empire-state had three very ambitious goals: 1) destruction of Austria-Hungary, with the Carpathian Mountains as Russia's new southwest border; 2) destruction of the Ottoman Empire and the annexation of the Bosphorus, the Dardanelles, Constantinople, and adjacent territory; and 3) the annexation of Armenia, Kurdistan, and Azerbaijan.

The Triple Entente (Great Britain, France, and Russia) opposed the three Central Powers (Germany, Austria-Hungary, and the Ottoman Empire). Russia's withdrawal after the communist revolution weakened the Triple Entente, but the USA provided a replacement empire-state. Troops from the USA tipped the balance on the Western Front and ended the stalemate. The Central Powers achieved a temporary victory on the Eastern Front, leading to the Treaty of Brest-Litovsk,[1] but the Central Powers collapsed when Germany lost on the Western Front. Victory on the Western Front and the withdrawal of Russia on the Eastern Front determined the post-war global order.

The war extinguished the *multilingual* Ottoman and Austro-Hungary empires. However, as a result of its withdrawal to consolidate its revolution, Russia did not achieve its territorial objectives. The victorious empires split the Austro-Hungarian Empire. The Ottoman Empire was divided into nation-states, with British and French zones of influence. Great Britain and France also divided the African colonial holdings of Germany. In World War I, empires defeated empires and the victorious empires reaped the spoils.

"Only three countries aspired to territorial expansion and war as a means to achieve it. They were Italy, Germany and Japan."

Niall Ferguson, *The War of the World:*
Twentieth-Century Conflict and the Descent of the West (2006)

2.1.2 <u>World War II: *Revisionist* Empires Defeated</u>. Germany, Italy, and Japan, the three *Versailles Treaty revisionists*, disrupted the *status quo* and precipitated World War II. They were three aggressively expansionist empires caught in a Thucydides Trap.[2] Aggressive bids for empire status, not fascist ideology,[3] created a security dilemma for the *status quo* empires. The security dilemma, not ideology, made World War II inevitable.

---

[1] This treaty, and the subsequent defeat of the Central Powers, was a major boon to the prevalence of the nation-state model. Estonia, Finland, Georgia, Latvia, Lithuania, Poland, and Ukraine gained independence.

[2] A reference to war between Sparta, a *status quo* power, and Athens, an emergent power. The rise of Athens caused a security dilemma. Sparta felt pressured to act before Athens became powerful enough to overturn the *status quo*.

[3] Generic fascism was no more antithetical to liberal democracy than Russian communism. Fascist Spain and corporatist Portugal focused on consolidating domestic control and stayed out of the war, despite German support for Spain in its recent civil war. They were not interested in challenging the *status quo* empires. After the war, Portugal was a founding member of NATO.

All three revisionists lacked essential size and resources, within their borders, for successful competition with the world's *status quo* empires. This was particularly the case for oil. Most oil extraction occurred in the Western Hemisphere. The Middle East produced one-tenth as much. The British, French, and Dutch colonial empires—along with two empire-states, the USA and USSR—monopolized the world supply of many essential commodities. To become competitive, Germany, Italy, and Japan were determined to acquire both space and natural resources. They knew the *status quo* empires would oppose their expansion. Mobilization sufficient to overcome this opposition required a fascist ideology.

Fascism was deemed necessary because of the emergence of *total warfare* during World War I. Total mobilization was perceived as essential and could best be realized with fascism. Fascism refers to the organization of a state on the principle of full mobilization of all resources, including human resources, and is generally established to permit aggressive expansion.[4] Such a state is autocratic and depersonalizing in exactly the same way as a military organization is. All Germans, Italians, and Japanese were, at least metaphorically, conscripted for total warfare by the fascist ideology.

Germany. After being stripped of its overseas territory in the Treaty of Versailles, Germany's ambition for empire focused on a large, contiguous, and German-speaking empire-state at the center of Europe. Germany appreciated that an empire-state was stronger than a colonial empire. Otto Von Bismarck's Prussian-dominated *Kleindeutschland* (Lesser Germany) was to be replaced by a *Grossdeutschland* (Greater Germany) that even incorporated large areas without a significant German population. Slavic populations were to be subjugated or replaced by Germans.

The German goal was to acquire *Lebensraum* (living space) through eastward expansion at the expense of the Slavs. The *status quo* empires could not permit Hitler to succeed, at least not beyond the acquisition of the German-speaking Sudetenland and Austrian Anschluss (joining).

---

[4] Sadly, pathologic expressions of racism and xenophobia can coexist with almost any ideology.

Invading Slavic Poland was unacceptably destabilizing. The status powers needed to respond.

Hitler allied himself with two other Versailles Treaty revisionists who also saw the necessity of a fascist ideology to mobilize for total war. Italy and Japan were building their own disruptive empires, respectively in the Mediterranean and Pacific.

Italy. Despite being on the winning side in World War I, post-war Italy was a Versailles Treaty revisionist. It had not gotten the Austro-Hungarian territory it had been promised in the secret 1915 Treaty of London. That promise had convinced it to leave the Triple Alliance and join the Triple Entente. Thus, it felt betrayed by France and Great Britain.

When Mussolini came to power in 1922, he formalized Italian control of Libya and sought Italian hegemony in the Mediterranean. Mussolini saw Italy as imprisoned in the Eastern Mediterranean by France and Great Britain. His ambition was unfettered access to the Atlantic—controlled by Great Britain at Gibraltar—and to the Indian Ocean—controlled by France at the Suez Canal. In addition, Corsica, Tunisia, Malta, and Cyprus gave the French and British an unacceptable dominance in the Mediterranean basin. Mussolini also coveted the African coast of the Mediterranean, Ethiopia, the Horn of Africa, the Dalmatian Coast, the Balkans, Greece, and Macedonia. His ambition can only be understood as a desire to establish a new Roman Empire.

"Modernity and industrialization in an era without free trade demanded Japan become an empire."

Peter Zeihan, *Disunited Nations:*
The Scramble for Power in an Ungoverned World (2020)

Japan. At the end of the 19th century, nearly half of the world's population and land area were under the jurisdiction of European colonial empires—Belgium, Great Britain, the Netherlands, France, Germany, Italy, Portugal, and Spain. Adding the three empire-states, Russia, China and the USA, it was clear that empires were the basis of global order. Japan saw its future in stark terms—become an empire or become a colony. Japan's empire-building began with four military victories: the First Sino–Japanese War, assistance in the suppression of the Boxer Rebellion, the Russo–Japanese War, and World War I (like Italy as a member of the Triple Entente).

The First Sino–Japanese War (Qing–Japan War) in 1894–95 ended in a Japanese victory and the Treaty of Shimonoseki. It gave Japan control of Korea, Taiwan, the Penghu Islands, and the Liaodong Peninsula. The Liaodong Peninsula was ceded back, as a result of pressure from Russia, France, and Germany. Their interest in exploiting China caused them to oppose what they considered excessive Japanese influence. The forced relinquishment of the fruits of war convinced Japan that its perceived need for an Asian empire required a showdown with Europe's colonial empires.

Allied with the Triple Entente in World War I, victory only gave Japan possession of the formerly German-controlled islands in the Western Pacific. Useful as these were for the Japanese Navy, they did not represent a significant territorial gain. Particularly galling for Japan was the rejection of its proposal that the Treaty of Versailles include a provision for racial equality in all member states of the League of Nations (LON). The limitation to LON members avoided an objection by the colonial empires, as their colonies would not be members. However, the provision for racial equality was blocked by the USA and Australia. Like Italy, an insufficient return on its war effort made Japan a Versailles Treaty revisionist.

In September 1931, after engineering the Mukden incident,[5] Japan invaded Manchuria and established a puppet state (Manchukuo) to permit Japanese occupation and mass migration. The invasion created a problem for the LON, as Japan was a member of its governing Council. It took the

---

[5] On September 18, 1931, a small bomb destroyed a section of the Japanese-owned South Manchuria Railway. Although the explosion was the work of Japanese troops who were ostensibly guarding the railway, Japan claimed it was a Chinese attack and used it as a pretext for the invasion of Manchuria.

LON a year to investigate and issue a report. In that year, Japan consolidated its position in Manchuria. The report found that the Mukden incident was a Japanese aggression and the LON Assembly demanded that Japan withdraw. Japan refused and left the LON. Stronger sanctions were not imposed.[6] The LON did nothing further.

Japan wanted to fight only China and Europe's Asian colonies. This seemed possible because the European powers were preoccupied by the war in Europe and the USA was preoccupied with its recovery from the Great Depression. Japan knew that conflict with the USA, China, and the European colonial empires would be more than it could handle.

On July 2, 1940, Congress authorized President Roosevelt to institute export restrictions on strategic goods and natural resources. A year later, on July 26, 1941 Roosevelt froze Japan's assets in the USA. On August 1, Roosevelt embargoed the oil and gasoline shipments that Japan needed to sustain its expansion.[7] The British and Dutch governments, which controlled the oil fields in Asia, joined the oil and gas embargo in the hope that Japan would see the futility of continuing its quest for an Asian empire. Japan, however, saw no future without an empire.

Japan realized it could not establish an Asian empire if it limited its ambition to what was acceptable to the *status quo* empires. The only hope for success appeared to be a series of quick and decisive victories, achieving temporary naval dominance in the Pacific and securing the British and Dutch oil fields in Asia. Japan's desperate gambit was initiated at Pearl Harbor on December 7, 1941. The final alignment in World War II

---

[6] The LON had authority for three types of sanctions: verbal, economic and physical. It only used the verbal.

[7] The timing of the embargo was crucial to preventing the Japanese from attacking Russia in Siberia. In the early Fall of 1941, Operation Barbarossa was reaching its zenith on Russia's Western Front and a coordinated Japanese attack in Siberia could drive Russia out of the war. By embargoing oil and gasoline, Roosevelt forced the Japanese to attack the oil producing regions in South East Asia rather than invade Siberia.

was three Versailles Treaty revisionists against all of the *status quo* empires and their colonies.

2.1.3 The Cold War: *Colonial* Empires Collapse.

After World War II, the colonial empire model was mortally wounded but still breathing. Even though it had recently been allied with Great Britain and France, the political and economic interests of the USA were better served by stripping the European powers of their colonies and reducing them to nation-state allies. Supporting colonialism was impossible because Europe's rebellious colonies were potential allies in the global contest with the USSR.

> "Moreover, American policy-makers, Roosevelt in particular, harbored a thinly veiled ambition to see the British Empire broken up."
> Niall Ferguson, *The War of the World: Twentieth-Century Conflict and the Descent of the West* (2006)

Prior to Pearl Harbor, there was little reason for the USA to save either the British and French colonial empires or the equally closed USSR. President Franklin D. Roosevelt's opposition to colonial empires was clear. Four months before the USA entered World War II, President Roosevelt and Prime Minister Churchill held their first wartime meeting on August 14, 1941. Afterward, they issued a "Joint Declaration" of eight principles for a post-war world order. It became known as The Atlantic Charter. At Roosevelt's insistence, the third principle of the charter was a declaration of opposition to colonialism:

> "Third, they respect the right of *all* peoples to choose the form of government under which they live; and they wish to see sovereign rights and self-government restored to those who have been forcibly deprived of them." (Emphasis added.)

Despite the plain meaning of the word *all*, there was no real meeting of the minds. Roosevelt did not want the USA to expend its citizens' lives and resources to make the world safe for either colonialism or communism. Churchill only agreed to the third principle under the pressure of Great Britain's reliance on the USA for war material and credit. An immediate domestic outcry forced Churchill to declare that it was his understanding that the right of self-determination should only apply in the territories of the fascist powers. It did not, he asserted, apply to the British Empire and, by logical extension, its European allies.

> "There never has been, there is not now, and there never will be any race on earth fit to serve as masters of their fellow man … any nationality, no matter how small, has the inherent right to its own neighborhood."
>
> President Franklin D. Roosevelt, White House
> Correspondents Dinner (March 15, 1941)

When Japan attacked the USA, differences among the allies about the territorial applicability of the right to self-determination were deferred for the duration. Even then, the USA did not declare war on Germany and Italy—only on Japan. The interests of the USA were still not sufficiently aligned with those of the European colonial empires or the USSR. Only when Germany and Italy declared war on the USA did the interests align—but only for the duration of the war.

Immediately after the war, the interests of the European colonial empires and the USSR aligned in opposition to self-determination. The Paris Peace Treaties of 1947 took a cynically realistic and pragmatically *ad hoc* approach to establishing boundaries and spheres of influence. President Truman, who replaced President Roosevelt, was no more successful after World War II than President Wilson had been on the issue of self-determination after World War I. However, this time, the colonial empires could not be salvaged.[8]

The Suez Crisis. After supporting the European colonial powers

---

[8]   The USA also had colonies. However, it was an empire-state and did not fight for what it did not need. The Philippine Independence Act of 1934 already provided for its sovereignty. Guam, American Samoa, and Puerto Rico were still useful to the military and incapable of revolution. They were small and economically dependent, so their status remained unchanged. In 1959, Hawaii became the 50th state of the USA.

in two global wars, colonial subjects were more aware of the limits of Europe's power. The two world wars also increased the colonial subjects' solidarity, self-confidence, and desire for independence.

The weakness of Europe's colonial empires and the continued antipathy toward them by the USA were starkly revealed in the 1956 Suez Crisis. In response to Egypt's acquisition of the stock of the privately owned Suez Canal in a forced sale, Great Britain and France conspired with Israel to recover the canal. The plan required Israel to secure the canal in a military action against Egypt, after which Great Britain and France would use the ruse of separating the combatants as a pretext to recover the canal. President Eisenhower learned of the plan and warned Great Britain not to proceed. He was ignored.

To the surprise of the British, after the fighting started the USA threatened to liquidate its massive holdings of British bonds. This would raise the borrowing cost for Great Britain to an unsustainable level. Considering the potential impact on its weak economy, Great Britain was forced into a humiliating withdrawal. France could not proceed alone. Israel, after negotiating access rights to the canal and the Straits of Tiran, withdrew in March 1957.

After the Suez Crisis, except for delusional elements in colonial offices and the military, the world knew that Europe's colonial empires were unsustainable. The Cold War competition for global influence and allies made both the USA and USSR hostile to colonialism. After the Suez crisis, the British were the most realistic and attempted to negotiate extended withdrawals. However, when rebuffed by successful independence movements, they left. The Portuguese, having avoided the weakening effects of World War II by abstaining, were the most recalcitrant colonialists and were not ejected from Africa until 1975.

In summary, 20th-century military conflicts caused a splintering of the contiguous but multilingual Austro-Hungarian and Ottoman empires after World War I, the defeat of the Versailles Treaty revisionists in World War II and the collapse of Europe's *colonial* empires during the Cold

War. The two World Wars demonstrated that the empire-state model was superior to both the nation-state model and to a variety of empires that could not compete with the empire-states.

2.1.4 <u>Post-Cold War: An *Ideological* Empire Dissolves</u>. The Cold War balance of power between two dominant empire-states used ideology to build alliances. Realists argue that the ideological debate was merely an organizational tool that masked an underlying great power rivalry. At the end of the 20th Century, the Cold War's bipolar order collapsed. The subsequent failure of Russia and China to integrate into the newly hegemonic world order and their current assertiveness lends credence to the Realist viewpoint. Alternatively, the Cold War had two fault lines (empire and ideology) and the victory of capitalism only resolved one of them.[9]

During the unipolar moment between the collapse of USSR and the rise of the Chinese empire-state, the Eastern European allies of the USSR availed themselves of the opportunity to escape Russian suzerainty. The Warsaw Pact nation-states, a coerced counterpart of NATO, dissolved on July, 1, 1991. All of its members then switched sides and became members of NATO.[10] Most of the Warsaw Pact's members, excluding only Albania, became members of the EU. Albania applied for EU membership but has not yet been accepted.

> "The central challenge to U.S. prosperity and security is the reemergence of long-term, strategic competition by what the National Security Strategy classifies as revisionist powers."
>
> Summary of the 2018 National Defense
> Strategy of the United States of America

---

[9] More likely, it resolved neither of them. The difference between market capitalism and state capitalism was the real dichotomy between economic systems during the latter stages of the Cold War.

[10] Albania, Bulgaria, Czechoslovakia (now Czechia and Slovakia), Hungary, Poland, Romania and East Germany (now part of Germany).

2.2 Making the Empire-States Great Again

The collapse of the 20th Century's bipolar order (Cold War) made the liberal democratic ideology of the victorious empire-state (USA) and its allies the basis for a potentially global order. During the period of liberal democratic hegemony, the military allies of the USA were its strongest economic competitors. Since economic strength is essential for long term international agency, the EU's economic competition undermined the NATO security alliance. The Cold War's hierarchy and implicit suzerainty was no longer viable.

After the 2008-2009 financial crisis, China and Russia saw market capitalism as prone to periodic crises that made it incompatible with their authoritarian political systems. Although Russia joined the WTO in 2012, great power competition reemerged with two revisionist empire-states, both autocratic, balancing against one *status quo* empire-state and its allies. Europe pursued its own economic interests and agenda while trying to preserve the benefits of the NATO subsidy of their security interests.

Nothing shows the dominance of the empire-state model as clearly as the re-emergence of China and Russia as revisionist empire-states. Three autonomous empire-states replaced the Cold War's two empire-state dominated networks. Europe fantasized about achieving international agency based solely on the size of its economy, without incurring the costs and political convergence necessary for the practice of collective high politics (security and foreign relaions).

"From this day forward, it's going to be only America first. America first. Every decision on trade, on taxes, on immigration, on foreign affairs will be made to benefit American workers and American families …. Protection will lead to greater prosperity and strength."

Donald Trump, First Inaugural Address (January 20, 2017)

2.2.1 <u>Make America Great Again</u>. Donald Trump, in his 2016 presidential campaign, used the slogan "Make America Great Again (MAGA)." It resonated with people whose focus was domestic and whose interests were poorly served, at least in relative terms, by globalization. MAGA was understood to prioritize their domestic interests over heritage relationships with former allies. It was a call for reducing the expense of maintaining a global order that Trump characterized as subsidizing the security of economic competitors who were feckless and free-riding defense allies.

Contentious economic relations with both China and the EU amplified Trump's message that the USA needed individual greatness, based entirely on self-interest and unburdened by global responsibility. It will be hard, if not impossible, for the post-Trump administration of President Joe Biden to reestablish the hierarchy that existed during the Cold War.[11] Nor is it likely that the EU will find any hierarchy acceptable, if its terms are satisfactory to the USA. The world seems destined to become multipolar, with the empire-states seeking regional and, if possible, transregional hegemony.

> "What does China's President Xi Jinping want? Four years before Donald Trump became president, Xi became the leader of China and announced an epic vision to, in effect, 'make China great again'—calling for 'the great rejuvenation of the Chinese nation.'"
>
> Graham Allison, *The Atlantic* (May 31, 2017)

2.2.2 <u>Make China Great Again</u>. China lost its position as the Middle Kingdom in the 19th Century, as a result of European imperialism. This loss of international agency was compounded by Japanese colonialism in the first half of the 20th Century. In the 21st Century, China is consciously attempting to regain regional hegemony and become a global

---

[11] Russia's revanchist aggression in Ukraine has increased EU and NATO solidarity. Even so, the leaders of France and Germany felt the need to engage in personal diplomacy with President Putin.

power second-to-none. It responded to its "century of humiliation" with a foreign relations policy of Realism and Great Power competition.

In 2001 China joined the WTO, but its subsequent interactions with other members have been transactional and legalistic. Since China's legal and economic systems are opaque, monitoring its compliance is difficult and China's state capitalism is seen by many in the West as incompatible with the basic premises of the *status quo* economic order and the rules of the WTO.

> "It seems clear that the United States erred in supporting China's entry into the WTO on terms that have proven to be ineffective in securing China's embrace of an open, market-oriented trade regime."
>
> *US Trade Representative 2017 Report to Congress on China's WTO Compliance* (January 2018)

Chairman Xi has a vision of a multi-centric world order that does not rely on the Bretton Woods institutions. Instead, Chairman Xi believes that the Middle Kingdom will become the world's largest economy and, consequently, the center of a global order that reflects both China's historic hegemony in Asia and importance on the Eurasian continent. For the 21st Century Eurasian order envisioned by Chairman Xi, the USA can only be an offshore balancer with limited capacity to affect the Eurasian balance of power.

Long before Trump, adopted the "Great Again" slogan, China's goal was to Make China Great Again. Regional preeminence, including the recovery of Taiwan, is China's immediate priority. This is normal empire-state behavior.

2.2.3 <u>Make Russia Great Again</u>. President Vladimir Putin called the collapse of the USSR "the greatest geopolitical catastrophe of the 20th Century" and is committed to the restoration of Russia's greatness. Long before President Trump was elected, President Putin was committed to "Make Russia Great Again." The results is an aggressively revanchist agenda.

The only way for Russia to reverse the "geopolitical catastrophe" of the collapse of the USSR and Warsaw Pact is to undermine both NATO and the EU. The EU, acting on behalf of more than two dozen countries, is often slow or unable to act collectively despite the knowledge that Russia is committed to its collapse. The EU lacks the coherence necessary to achieve the political integration necessary to orchestrate European high politics or overcome its members economic nationalism. The lack of EU coherence brings us to the subject of Part II: Congruence is Essential.

Part II

Congruence is Essential

"A common language connects the members of a community into an information sharing network with formidable collective powers."

Stephen Pinker, The Language Instinct (1994)

Chapter 3

Congruence in the Nation-State Model

Linguistic congruence in the empire-states is the "magic sauce" in their recipe for global agency. India's needs congruence in order to become the fourth empire-state. The EU and AU need linguistic congruence in their respective inchoate region-states. Monolingualism is not an option. Bilingual congruence is the only option. Understanding the global need for bilingual congruence begins with a look at what Stephen Pinker describes as "information sharing network[s] with formidable collective powers" and the history of monolingual congruence.

> "In short, bonding and bridging are not 'either-or' categories into which social networks can be neatly divided, but 'more or less' dimensions along which we can compare different forms of social capital."
>
> Robert D. Putnam, *Bowling Alone* (2001)

3.1 Language Networks: The Two Functions of Languages

Human languages, as opposed to the rudimentary communication in other species, are an essential characteristic of our species. It is not surprising, then, that languages are powerful markers for differentiating "us" from "them." This reflects the identity function of a language. Shared identities bond people and different identities separate them. If religion, history, and culture are variables, a common language may be the principal basis for cohesion in pluralistic societies. Thankfully, it can be potent enough to succeed.

3.1.1 The Communication Function: Bridge Languages.

For people from different language communities to interact, a bridge language is needed. Communication with a bridge language does not invoke a common identity, although it can increase understanding, respect, and empathy. This contrasts with a common birth language, which unites the communication function with an identity function.

Pidgins, Creoles, and Lingua Franca. Bridge languages come in two flavors: pidgins and *lingua franca*. A pidgin is a hybrid of two or more languages that is negotiated by speakers from different language communities. In contrast, a *lingua franca* is any available language that can be used as a bridge language. Today, because a *lingua franca* is almost always available, pidgins are rarely created.

Pidgins and Creoles. A pidgin is created when there is regular contact between different language communities and no common language is available. It only develops to the extent necessary for specific objectives, such as trade. There are no native speakers of a pidgin. True pidgins are now rare, but some languages that began as pidgins are still called "Pidgin." This reflects their origin, but they have become creole languages. Unless it becomes a creole language, a pidgin will last no longer than the circumstances that motivated its creation.

If a pidgin is their primary means of communication, children in a linguistically diverse community can elaborate it to meet all their needs. By the time they become adults, the pidgin will have expanded into a complete language, which is called a creole. Locally, it may partially or completely displace one or more of its source languages. This is common when the source languages communities are diasporas, as was the case in the creation of many plantation creoles.

Lingua franca. The proper name *Lingua Franca* means Language of the Franks and refers to a pidgin that was used in Mediterranean trade for centuries. The generic term *lingua franca* came into use much later and refers to any language that is used as a communication bridge. It can be the first language of some people using it or a second language for all. If the *lingua franca* is the first language of some users, they have a major advantage (e.g., English in Europe). This is why most Europeans do not want the EU to privilege the language of any EU member state.

Although only a few languages are widely used as *lingua franca*, learning any language makes it available as a *lingua franca* bridge for communication with its other speakers. In a world with thousands of languages, knowing a major *lingua franca* is very useful, especially for the members of smaller language communities.

"The current champion learning algorithm for machine translation is a form of so-called deep learning, and it produces a rule in the form of an artificial neural network with hundreds of layers and millions of parameters."

Stuart Russell, *Human Compatible* (2019)

Replacing *Lingua Franca:* Machine Translation Technology (MTT). The EU Commission, one of the world's largest governmental users of MTT, has an online MTT service. The EU Council also has an MTT program called the *EU Council Presidency Translator*. On August 3, 2020, the European Parliament selected a company to automatically transcribe and translate parliamentary debates in all 24 official languages in real time. The UN, with 75% fewer official languages (6:24), is pursuing a similar translation initiative jointly with the World Intellectual Property Organization. In the private sector, Meta (Facebook) provides more than 20 billion translations per day in 160 different languages just for its News Feed.

For optimists, MTT is seen as providing access to greater diversity, which will broaden the outlook of its users. This replicates the optimistic view of the Internet in its early years. The Internet was expected to create broader communities and make users less xenophobic. The reality is sometimes the creation of geographically dispersed but culturally narrow silos that are echo chambers and amplifiers for narrow perspectives and interests. Unintended consequences are ubiquitous with advances in technology. Undoubtedly, MTT will facilitate new *transactional* encounters. Tourists will be able to venture further from resorts and other traditional tourist destinations. However, transactional encounters are not as important as personal relationships.

Some benefits of learning a *lingua franca* will disappear in the next two decades. Fewer jobs will require plurilingualism, as translations will accurately and more economically be supplied by MTT. Why should employers pay a premium for bilingual employees when technology provides a more cost-effective alternative? As the benefits decline, so will the motivation to learn a "foreign" language. Why should students spend countless hours trying to learn a language, often with little success, when MTT can provide the capacity with an inexpensive application?

The undeniable effect of MTT will be the separation of languages' communication function from their identity function. Complementary bilingualism, with two mother tongues and an assist from MTT for transactional communication, is a better future. It will create broader identities and increase both understanding (communication) and empathy (identity). An easily learned language in a policy of 2MT complementary bilingualism will produce greater unity within future region-states and India. It can even produce a global community of communication with an inclusive identity.

"The emotional investment in the Chinese language, for those who have known it all their lives, is synonymous with being Chinese."
Jing Tsu, *Sound and Script in Chinese Diaspora* (2010)

3.1.2 The Identity Function: Bonding Languages. There are at least four ways for an identity to be attached to a language. 1) mother tongue (MT) identity, including a bilingual 2MT identity pair, 2) a pidgin can become a creole, 3) part of a language community can differentiate its language use to create a more distinct identity, and 4) a linguistically heterogeneous population can converge on a single choice to become a unified language community.

"Men and women do not choose collective identification as they chose shoes, knowing that one could only put on one pair at a time."
Eric Hobsbawm, *Nations and Nationalism Since 1780* (1990)

Adding the Identity Function: From Pidgin to Creole. The capacity to create a pidgin and elaborate it into a creole was documented at two government schools in Nicaragua that taught deaf students. Until the late 1970s, the deaf had no community. They used gestures that were created independently by each family. In 1977, a program for deaf children of elementary school age was established in Managua. In 1980, a vocational school for deaf adolescents was added.

These schools achieved modest success in their explicit goals of teaching written Spanish and lip reading. Spontaneously, in the schoolyard and going to and from school, the children taught themselves to communicate with gestures. It was a signing pidgin, a hybrid negotiated from their family signs.

Unable to understand the students' signing, the faculty asked for help and the Ministry of Education contacted the Massachusetts Institute of Technology (MIT). A graduate student from MIT documented the students' signing and discovered that the *younger* students had a larger vocabulary and used a more complex grammar than the older students. Students who started school as adolescents usually stopped progressing once they acquired the pidgin. Younger students, exposed to the pidgin during the years when children learn a first language, playfully experimented and expanded the pidgin into a creole and became a normal language community. The pidgin of the older students was named Lenguaje de Signos Nicaragüense (LSN), and the creole created by the younger students was named Idioma de Señas de Nicaragua (ISN).

Adding the Identity Function: Divergence. When people who share a language want to create distinct communities, divergence in language use establishes distinct identities. My favorite example of identity by divergence involves the intentional creation of a new dialect in Papua New Guinea. A group within the Buin language community created the Uisai dialect by switching the markers for words in different grammatical gender categories. This simple change was startling to speakers of standard Buin, and consequently, created a distinct identity for its users.

Divergence after Standardization. Identity by divergence is currently occurring in the Balkans in the aftermath of the breakup of Yugoslavia. Change began with standardization in the 19th century. In the late 20th century, convergence was reversed to express different identities.

Historically, language use in the Balkans was a Slavic continuum. In the middle of the 19th century the literate elite championed standardization. Serbian and Croatian writers and academics created a standard that was based on the Slavic dialect spoken in Zagreb. Standardization would facilitate the printing and sale of books. The proposed standard was published in 1850 as the *Vienna Literary Agreement*, which unified a written language.

After World War I, the Kingdom of the Serbs, Croats, and Slovens, renamed Yugoslavia in 1929, used the standard of the *Vienna Literary Agreement* as its written language. For the average and often illiterate person, the Slavic continuum was still their linguistic environment. In 1941, Germany occupied Yugoslavia. The anti-Nazi resistance ignored the elite written standard, as partisans came primarily from the less literate agricultural communities. After World War II, the newly established Socialist Federal Republic of Yugoslavia initially recognized multiple dialects, rather than privileging one of them.

In 1954, Yugoslavia's writers and academicians renewed the call for standardization. In a declaration called the *Novi Sad Agreement*, they insisted on a single language, called Serbo-Croatian, with two dialects: Western (Zageb) and Eastern (Belgrade). It could be written in either the Latin or Cyrillic script. Serbo-Croatian was adopted by the communist government because language rationalization was now appreciated as useful for both increasing literacy (communication) and citizen solidarity (identity).

Subsequent Divergence. In March 1967, 130 influential Croatian writers and academicians, expressing an ethnolinguistic identity, published the *Declaration on the Status and Name of the Croatian Literary Language*. Unlike the authors of the *Vienna Literary Agreement* and the *Novi Sad Agreement*, they advocated distinct languages. Many were Croatian nationalists who were upset that Croatian was treated as a provincial dialect. They wanted a Croatian identity language.

President Tito employed the necessary force to suppress nationalism, but he could not extinguish ethnolinguistic aspirations. To defuse tension, a new constitution in 1974 dramatically decentralized Yugoslavia's government. Authority and responsibility were significantly transferred to regions, with the federal government retaining limited powers. This devolution considerably increased the congruence between linguistic communities and the institutions of governance.

The 1974 changes facilitated the dissolution of Yugoslavia in the 1990s. Skipping the details, the result was four official languages: Croatian, Bosnian, Serbian, and Montenegrin. As the written form of all four languages is based on the Serbo-Croatian of the Novi Sad Agreement and the Vienna Literary Agreement, they can be seen as variants of one polycentric language. That is not, however, how the users perceive them. The languages are becoming identity languages for distinct communities, and variations are continually accreting to make them increasingly distinct.

Adding the Identity Function by Convergence: Hebrew in Palestine. Convergence is generally a result of the creation of a nation-state. However, even without a government policy, a linguistically diverse group can become a unified community by converging on a single language. One non-governmental example is the revival of Hebrew by Jewish settlers in Palestine.

The revival of written Hebrew for publishing was a project of the literary elite in the Ashkenazi diaspora. The subsequent addition of an identity function occurred in Palestine, where the language moved from print to the street. The revival of Hebrew in Palestine is usually divided into three periods: the First (Farmers) Aliyah, the Second Aliyah, and the British Mandate. In some agricultural settlements of the First Aliyah, notably in Rishon LeZion circa 1886, schools taught Hebrew and used it as the language of instruction for some classes. However, both Ashkenazi and Sephardic dialects were used without standardization. To address this problem, in 1890, the Hebrew Language Committee (*Va'ad ha-Lashon ha-'Ivrit*) was established to standardize spoken Hebrew.

In the Second Aliyah, there was a strong desire to show commitment to *Eretz Israel* by consciously separating one's identity from the former life in the diaspora. This encouraged the use of Hebrew and it expanded into the public space, especially for gatherings that drew from multiple language communities. In 1909, Tel Aviv was established as a Jewish housing estate on the outskirts of the port city of Jaffa. In 1913, when the Company for the Aid of German Jews specified German as the language of instruction at a science and engineering school that they established in Tel Aviv, a backlash forced them to accept the use of Hebrew.

The third period of Hebrew's revival is marked by the end of the Ottoman Empire at the conclusion of World War I. In predominantly Jewish communities of the British Protectorate, the Legion of the Defenders of the Language used social pressure to get immigrants to learn Hebrew. Speaking any other language in public, even if merely overheard, could be met with a remonstration—"*Ivri, daber ivrit*" (Hebrews speak Hebrew). Thus, several decades before Israel was established in 1948, the groundwork was laid for Hebrew to be used as its identity language.

> "The strong European states that emerged in the nineteenth century were built around a national principle that made language and ethnicity the core of national identity."
>
> Francis Fukuyama, *Political Order and Political Decay* (2014)

3.2 Monolingual Congruence in Europe's Nation-States

While only marginally relevant to global order, except when destabilizing a region or as part of an alliance, nation-states are numerous. Nation-state prevalence, popularity, and resilience are attributable to the strength of their identities, which are based on linguistic congruence. French speak French. Germans speak German. The ideal form of a nation-state is "one-nation, one-state, one-language." The name of a country is often the same as that of its language, as a quick look at the map of Europe or the world will show.

There were two paths to achieving monolingual congruence in Europe: (1) *state-first*, which started with an existing state and established congruence by privileging a single language, and (2) *nation-first*, which drew a state boundary around an ethnolinguistic nation, real or imagined, and added the institutions of governance. In the second case, the circumscribed population was either monolingual or part of a language continuum. If dialect diversity persisted, as in Germany, there was uniformity in the written language. In both cases, monolingual congruence aligned a language community (demos-nation) with the institutions of governance (polity-state).

3.2.1 State-First Monolingual Congruence. The borders of many European states reflect a long dead monarch's ability to project military power and hold the territory acquired by inheritance, conquest, and dowry. If natural barriers were significant, the border would generally conform. State borders often fail to reflect the distribution of language communities. Thus, because both the Catalan and Basque communities cross the Pyrenees, each is a minority community in both France and Spain.

France (Top-Down). In monarchies, language use concerned only the elite and language rationalization often began as a project of the literate minority to establish a written standard for printing books. For example, the Académie Francaise began as a group of distinguished French citizens who were interested in establishing standards for printing in French. In 1635, it was co-opted by Cardinal Richelieu, first minister of King Louis

XIII, and tasked with creating a dictionary and grammar for standard French. Cardinal Richelieu's objective was to consolidate the king's power by establishing a bureaucracy of lesser nobles and literate commoners (*intendants* and *subdélégués*) that used a standardized vernacular. Bureaucrats were geographically rotated to reduce provincial influence on them. A dependent bureaucracy that used a common vernacular language diminished the power of both the high nobility and the clergy.

"The French Revolution had, moreover, unleashed not just demands for popular political participation but also a new form of identity by which a shared language and culture would be the central source of unity for the new democratic public."

Francis Fukuyama, *Political Order and Political Decay* (2014)

Revolutionary France. The revolution of 1789 changed France dramatically. The adoption of a policy of territorial monolingualism was one of the most radical changes. A common language was deemed essential to consolidate and sustain the revolution because the revolutionary government needed to communicate its authority and political message to each citizen. Minority language communities were often rural, religious, and politically conservative. These qualities made them ripe for counter-revolutionary efforts; thus, the continued use of a regional language or dialect became a marker for failing to fully embrace the revolutionary order. For the first time, the language used by the people mattered to the government.

"One can assure without exaggeration that at least 6 million Frenchmen, especially in the provinces, are ignorant of the national language; that an equal number is incapable of holding a sustained conversation; that in the last analysis the number of those who speak it fluently does not exceed 3 million …."

Abbé Henri Grégoire, *Report to the National Convention* (1794)[12]

---

[12] The quotation from Abbé Henri Grégoire is well known. Less well known is that he added: "… the important thing is that all Frenchmen understand and speak the national language without forgetting their individual dialects." He was an early advocate of what this essay calls complementary bilingualism.

In the first week of June 1794, an important document was submitted to the revolutionary government by Abbé Henri Grégoire, who had been in charge of the 1790 census. The following was its descriptive title: "On the Necessity and Means for Eliminating Dialects and Universalizing the Use of the French Language." The same year, laws were enacted to require the use of standard (*Ile de France*) French in public affairs.

Napoleonic France. The territorial monolingualism that the revolution established in principle, but lacked the time and resources to implement, was subsequently advanced by Napoleon's military adventures. The Napoleonic Wars showed that a monolingual army performed better in combat. Speaking a common language avoided misunderstanding orders. Patriotism, based in part on an ethnolinguistic identity, improved military performance. While Napoleon's army units were initially composed of soldiers from a single area and some units even used a regional language or a nonstandard dialect, replacements were assigned as needed and without regard to the dialect spoken by the replacement or by the unit to which they were assigned. As the campaigns consumed soldiers, the units became increasingly reliant on standard French.

Modern France. From the 1880s, France mandated primary school education in standard French. The effects of the printing press, French revolution, Napoleonic conscription, and universal education were combined to complete the transition from the *laissez-faire* multilingualism of feudalism to the monolingualism of a modern nation-state.

Precisely how long it took for France to become monolingual is difficult to determine. After the sobering revelation of the 1790 census, questions on language usage were dropped from subsequent surveys. However long it took, the results are clear: the French have great affection for their language. For example, to blunt the influence of the 1992 European Charter of Regional or Minority Languages, France amended Article 2 of its constitution to specify the following: "The language of the Republic is French." Not that there was any doubt, but the constitutional designation of a single official language impeded efforts to establish minority language rights.[13]

England (Bottom-Up). Establishing state-first congruence in Great Britain proceeded very differently. Linguistic congruence in France was top-down. English congruence was bottom-up. English became hegemonic because the Anglo-Norman feudal aristocracy needed to align its identity with the masses in order to win their support for campaigns to seize territory in France during the Hundred Years' War.

England and France were antagonistically intertwined for over seven centuries, from the Norman invasion in 1066 until 1811, when the British monarchs finally renounced all territorial claims in France. A milestone in the ascendency of English came in 1362, when Edward III broke a 300-year tradition of using French, dating back to the Norman Conquest, and addressed the Parliament in English. Bottom-up linguistic congruence was easier than trying to impose the Norman French language, especially as there was no educational infrastructure to support such an overwhelming enterprise.

> "Of all state simplifications, then, the imposition of a single, official language may be the most powerful, and it is the precondition of many other simplifications."
>
> James C. Scott, *Seeing Like a State* (1998)

3.2.2 Nation-First Monolingual Congruence. The second path to creating a nation-state drew a state boundary around a real or imagined nation, which was identified by the use of a common language or mutually comprehensible dialects. The nation-first model is exemplified by Germany.

Germany (Aggregation). Speakers of German dialects formed the core of the Holy Roman Empire (HRE)—which, however, included substantial

---

[13] The president of France signed the European Charter for Regional or Minority Languages in 1999. However, ratification was rejected by the legislative branch. Ratification was rejected a second time in 2015.

populations that spoke dialects of Czech, Slovene, Dutch, Polish, Italian, and French. Starting with a multilingual empire composed of hundreds of mini-states, considerable effort was required to carve out a monolingual German nation-state.

In the century after the Reformation of 1517, Lutheranism became the official religion in many northern pieces of the HRE. Roman Catholicism dominated in the South, so religious fault lines emerged. Eventually, a mix of religious intolerance and balance of power necessity led to Europe's Thirty Years' War (1618–48) and the death of one-third of the HRE's German-speaking population. When the slaughter ended in 1648, the Peace of Westphalia expanded religious liberty and established exclusive sovereignty within the defined state borders as well as the *de jure* equality of states under international law. States were no longer the private property of monarchs. The Peace of Westphalia was a search for a more stable order and the beginning of the European state system.

The Peace of Westphalia loosened Austrian control in the HRE and allowed Prussia to emerge as a rival for the leadership of the German-speaking people. The years between the Peace of Westphalia and the French Revolution saw Prussia assert itself in military conflicts, including the War of the Austrian Succession (1740–48) and the Seven Years' War (1756–63). In both cases, Prussia was part of the winning coalition and Austria was part of the losing coalition.

Napoleonic Consolidation. The multilingual HRE was the primary victim of the Napoleonic Wars. In 1805, at the Battle of Austerlitz, Napoleon's forces (including some allied German states) defeated the HRE. The following year, Emperor Francis II abdicated. Napoleon replaced the HRE with the Confederated States of the Rhine and, in the process, reduced the number of government units in the HRE from over 300 to just 16.[14]

---

[14] It later increased to 36. Ironically, Napoleon's consolidation benefited Germany more than he ever benefited France. Napoleon also did more for the USA, by the Louisiana Purchase, than he did for France.

The Confederated States of the Rhine only lasted for a decade. After Napoleon's disastrous winter in Russia, members began switching sides by joining the coalition that would defeat Napoleon. At the Congress of Vienna (1814–15), the leaders of the coalition did not want to re-establish the HRE, as German speakers were showing unmistakable signs of their collective power. Instead, the Vienna Treaties established a German Confederation of 39 sovereign states and included only portions of the former Austrian and Prussian territories. The goal was a European balance in which no government was powerful enough to act unilaterally.

Influenced by the Enlightenment, the French Revolution, and Napoleonic reforms, some states in the German Confederation drafted constitutions that included civil rights. There was a conservative backlash in the form of the Carlsbad Decrees, issued in 1819 by the Bundestag. The only central institution of the German Confederation, with its seat in Frankfurt, the Bundestag was a congress of the nobles' envoys. The liberal reaction to the Carlsbad Decrees led to more than a decade of sporadic unrest in various parts of the German Confederation.

In 1848, a series of liberal revolutions broke out across Europe, including France, Austria, and the German Confederation. In the German Confederation, the revolutions stressed both German nationalism and opposition to autocratic rule. The middle class demanded political rights with a lower property qualification, liberal policies, German unity, and a constitutional monarchy. The working class demanded better working conditions and universal male suffrage.

The combined strength of the middle class and working class cowed the German aristocracy and succeeded in replacing the Bundestag with a parliament. After 230 sessions, a compromise was reached, but it was between the conservatives and middle-class. It rejected the goals of the working class. The compromise was expressed in the Imperial Constitution of 1849. It provided for a bicameral parliament, adopted the "Lesser Germany" model, and established a constitutional monarchy. A provisional power replaced the German Confederation and the crown of a constitutional monarchy was offered to the Prussian King, Frederick Wilhelm I. It was anticipated that he would accept the offer, as the constitution decided the competition with Austria in favor of Prussia.

Surprisingly, at least to the middle-class, Wilhelm I declined the crown because of the constitution's limits on hereditary power. This sent a clear signal to the conservatives that their coalition with the middle-class should be abrogated. The earlier split, when the middle-class abandoned their working-class allies, now showed its significance. Division of the opposition permitted the Prussian military to suppress both the radical working class and the liberal middle class. The Frankfurt Parliament was dissolved. The German Confederation was reestablished.

From HRE to Kleindeutschland. Could the speakers of different German dialects, divided among dozens of governments, forge a single nation-state? An early proponent of an affirmative answer was the German philosopher Johann Fichte (1762–1814), who championed the idea that states must be ethnolinguistic communities. His belief in the imperative of a German-speaking nation-state was ardently expressed in an influential 1808 book, *Address to the German Nation*:

> "Those who speak the same language are joined to each other by a multitude of invisible bonds ... they understand each other and have the power of continuing to make themselves understood more and more clearly; they belong together and are by nature one and an inseparable whole."

Establishing a German nation-state required a resolution of the rivalry between German-speaking Prussia and multilingual Austria. Led by Prussia, most of the German Confederation, excluding Austria, formed a customs union in 1834 (Zollverein).[15] Prussia also championed the idea of

---

[15] This is an interesting parallel with the establishment of the EU customs union. The difference, of course, is the linguistic congruence in the case of the Zollverein. Congruence within the Zollverein presaged the subsequent political unity of Germany. A lack of the congruence may presage EU failure.

a monolingual Kleindeutschland (Lesser Germany) that excluded Austria and other multilingual areas of the confederation.[16]

Bismarck's Germany. In the decade after becoming the Minister President and Foreign Minister of Prussia in 1862, Otto von Bismarck engineered and won three wars that united 25 German-speaking states. The first war, in 1864, was against Denmark over control of Schleswig-Holstein, with a larger objective of demonstrating Prussian military power. The second war, in 1866, was against Austria and established Prussia as the leader of the German-speaking people.[17] In 1867, the German Confederation was replaced by a Northern German Confederation under Prussian leadership.

The third and final war of German unification was against France, in 1870, to bring the independent German-speaking states of Baden, Württemberg, Bavaria, and Hesse-Darmstadt into the Prussian fold.[18] During the shelling of Paris, with victory imminent, King Wilhelm I of Prussia was crowned as the emperor of Germany. The unification of Germany, based on the Lesser Germany model, established a monolingual nation-state using the nation-first model.

Czechia and Slovakia: (Decomposition). The aggregation process, used to create Germany, is not the only nation-first method. Decomposition can also produce a monolingual state. Among the most recent nation-first creations of monolingual nation-states in Europe, except for the still-evolving organization of the Balkans, was the 1993 breakup of Czechoslovakia into Czechia and Slovakia. This is interesting because, at the moment of the dissolution, it seemed to happen spontaneously. The political elite

---

[16] Even the Kleindeutschland was slightly over-inclusive. It included French speakers in Alsace-Lorraine (Metz-Château-Salins), Danish speakers in Northern Schleswig, and Polish speakers in Eastern Prussia.

[17] This allowed Italy to free Venice from Austrian control and add it to the Kingdom of Italy.

[18] This war allowed Italy to incorporate the Papal states, which had been under the protection of France. It completed both Italian unification and German unification.

chose to divide the country along a linguistic fault line, and the citizens responded with indifferent acceptance.

The history of Czechoslovakia that led up to its dissolution, however, shows that coercion and violence were required. The violent expulsion of German speakers after World War II is the most famous example. In 1968, Czechoslovakia unintentionally set the border for a future dissolution in the Constitutional Act on the Czechoslovak Federation. Three decades later, after the fall of communism, the natural line of separation was already established by the federation's internal ethnolinguistic boundaries.

The respective languages of the two new nation-states are Czech and Slovak, both of which are West Slavic languages and mutually intelligible in mundane daily conversations. The Czech language is now prescriptively regulated by the Institute of the Czech Language, and the Slovak language is similarly regulated by the Ľudovít Štúr Institute of Linguistics of the Slovak Academy of Sciences. Given the different identities and regulatory bodies, further divergence is inevitable.

3.3 Europe's Unexceptional Exceptions

Not all of Europe's nation-states achieved the ideal of combining one nation, one state, and one language. Europe's three exceptions are Luxembourg, Switzerland, and Belgium.[19] It is not a coincidence that all three are close neighbors on the fault line between Europe's Germanic- and Romance-language communities.

Despite the linguistic fault line running through them, all three have

---

[19] Other EU member states also have more than one official language. Ireland has English and Irish, but 93% consider English their mother tongue. In Malta, 97% consider Maltese their mother tongue, although English is also an official language. In Finland, only 5% consider the co-official Swedish their mother tongue. In Cyprus, the North speaks Turkish and the South speaks Greek. In each part there is congruence with a single language and, due to Turkey's invasion in 1974, very little cross community contact.

achieved *de facto* linguistic congruence. They are exceptions because they are multilingual but unexceptional because they have monolingual congruence below the surface (Switzerland and Belgium) or the linguistic congruence of a unitary trilingual community (Luxembourg). Their significance lies in not their overall multilingualism but the fact that they still achieved congruence between unified language communities and the institutions of governance.

3.3.1 Luxembourg: Equal Sets Congruence. With a population of approximately 600,000 and an area of just 2600 km2, tiny Luxembourg is a case in which three languages (German, French, and Luxembourgish) establish trilingual congruence. In mathematical terms, Luxembourg's language communities are equal sets.[20] There is still the essential congruence between a single (trilingual) demos with a unified polity.

Luxembourg is instructive because it demonstrates that a country can achieve trilingual congruence. Bilingual congruence will be 50% easier, with only one *additional* language. Here is some relevant background:

(1) Luxembourgish (Letzeburgesch) is the primary oral language. It is the default choice in less formal situations, such as daily encounters and text messaging. Its unified written form was first recognized in 1975. Luxembourgish had no official status until 1984, when it became the sole *national* language. Luxembourgish invokes the Luxembourg identity. This reflects a desire to be distinguished from the neighboring France and Germany. Along with German and French, it is one of the three *official* languages of Luxembourg.

(2) French is a prestigious language that primarily occupies functional domains. For example, French is the language of the legal system. All laws are enacted in French. This reflects the historic prestige of French and Luxembourg's adoption of the Napoleonic Code. However, in the

---

[20] Luxembourg citizens are trilingual in the same three languages: Luxembourgish 90% (77% native and 13% second language), German 92% (4% native and 88% second language), and French 96% (6% native and 90% second language). Thus, Luxembourg is linguistically unified.

Parliament, laws are generally introduced in German and debated in Luxembourgish.

(3) Newspapers are predominantly printed in German, but with French interspersed. French is more common in advertisements for luxury goods, wedding and birth announcements, and stories with a European or cultural focus.

(4) The broadcast media predominantly uses Luxembourgish; however, news is often presented in German or a mix of German and Luxembourgish.

(5) Government primarily writes in French or German, and only occasionally in Luxembourgish. However, a citizen's use of Luxembourgish is always accommodated. Luxembourgish dominates informal communication.

The key to Luxembourg's successful trilingualism is its school system. Teachers must be proficient in all three languages. The students are taught all three languages as subjects and all three languages are used as languages of instruction. Preschool and early elementary education is in Luxembourgish.[21] German replaces Luxembourgish in the elementary grades, as children are taught to read and write in German. In the early secondary school grades, German is used for all courses except science and mathematics, which are taught in French. In grades 10 and above, courses are generally in French. In some secondary schools, students transition to French earlier. Students who are tracked to a vocational education generally continue in German. At all levels and as needed, assistance is available in Luxembourgish.

Luxembourg is an exceptionally wealthy country, and its trilingual[22] model may be too expensive for other countries to adopt, except as an

---

[21] Prior to 1843, German was used in the primary grades and French was used in secondary education.

[22] English is a very popular fourth language. Luxembourg's plurilingualism is remarkable. In comparison, 2MT complementary bilingualism is a radically easier way to establish congruence - even global congruence.

aspirational goal. In addition, the cognitive load of three languages can displace other educational goals. Luxembourg also has a high dropout rate in its lower socio-economic and immigrant communities. It also directs a larger than average percentage of students to vocational education. Finally, it is very difficult for immigrants to assimilate into a trilingual community. The point is that unitary trilingualism is possible, so a much less difficult policy of 2 MT complementary bilingualism is practical.[23]

3.3.2 <u>Switzerland: Congruence by Segregation</u>. Switzerland is the country most often cited as an exception to Europe's monolingual nation-state model. However, the Swiss live in monolingual communities and language rights are territorial, not personal. If you move to a different part of Switzerland, you must use its official language when dealing with the government. Switzerland is linguistically segregated, with monolingual congruence behind the veneer of multilingualism. Citizens rarely relocate to a different language's territory.

"Switzerland may be quadrilingual, but to all intents and purposes each point of its territory can be viewed as unilingual."
Francois Grin, *Multilingualism and Government* (2000)

Most Swiss are either German speakers 2/3 or French speakers 1/4. Less than 10% are native speakers of Italian (8.4%) and Romansch (0.7%). Of Switzerland's 26 cantons, 22 have one official language (17 German, 4 French, and 1 Italian). Most government functions are performed by

---

[23] In South America, Paraguay has *de facto* congruence in Spanish and Guarani. In Paraguay, 90% of the population speaks Guarani and 87% speaks Spanish. This translates to at least 73% of the population speaking both languages. Unlike affluent Luxembourg, Paraguay ranks in the lower half of the world's nation-states on the basis of per capita GDP. Paraguay shows that bilingualism is not just for the affluent. It does not, at least yet, have a policy of complementary bilingualism. If it did, the results would be very positive for Guarani monolinguals and the speakers of all indigenous languages, many of which are in decline due to a shift to Guarani.

monolingual cantons or by monolingual districts and municipalities in the four multilingual cantons.

Of the four multilingual cantons, three are bilingual in German and French: Berne (Bern), Fribourg (Freiburg), and Valais (Wallis). Running through these three cantons, the linguistic fault line is commonly referred to as the *Röschtigraben*.[24] Congruence is achieved with monolingual districts and municipalities. For example, in Valais (Wallis), there are six French-speaking districts (Lower Valais) and eight German-speaking districts (Upper Wallis). In the Canton of Fribourg (Freiburg), the French districts are in the West and the German districts are in the East.

Similar internal linguistic territoriality exists in Berne (Bern). Jura bernois is the name of its Francophone area. At the risk of including too much information, the history of Francophone Berne and the birth of the Canton of Jura is instructive concerning the interaction of linguistic and religious cleavages. The Catholic and Francophone Jura region, which had previously not been a part of Switzerland, was added to the Canton of Bern at the Congress of Vienna (1815). Since Bern was Protestant and German speaking, this was problematic, but the ensuing dissension never achieved critical mass.

After the Second World War, in which France and Germany were both antagonists and collaborators (Vichy), a separatist movement emerged. In 1979 a new and Francophone Canton of Jura was created by separating out a Francophone portion of Bern (Berne). However, not all of Francophone Bern joined the new Canton of Jura. The areas that remained in Bern (Berne) were Francophone but not Catholic. They are called *Jura bernois*, which should not be confused with the Canton of Jura.

In Jura bernois (Bern) religious identity seemed to have trumped linguistic identity. It is also possible that the greater wealth and political importance of the more urban Bern tipped the balance. This balance,

---

[24] Röschti is a German dish made with grated potatoes. A Graben is a trench or other division.

however, proved unstable. Religion has become less salient relative to language. By 1994, the Francophone question reemerged and a decade later a federal commission proposed that Jura bernois be removed from the Canton of Bern and added to the Canton of Jura. On March 28, 2021, part of Jura bernois (Moutier) voted to leave Bern and join Jura.[25] This change is scheduled to occur in 2026.

Even the trilingual Graubünden (Grisons) Canton is largely segregated by language. For example, Italian speakers live in the South, in four of the canton's 11 districts (Moesa, Bernina, the municipality of Bivo in Albula, and the municipality of Bregaglia in Maloja). Many of the residents in these districts commute for work to the adjacent Canton of Ticino, where Italian is the sole official language. Moreover, many Italian speakers born in Grisons relocate to Ticino.[26]

3.3.3 <u>Belgium: Incomplete Congruence</u>. Like Switzerland, to achieve linguistic congruence, Belgium combines monolingual territoriality and devolution. It is able to do this because its language communities are largely self-segregated. Dutch (Flemish) speakers live in the North (Flanders) and French speakers live in the South (Wallonia). The very small German-speaking population (<1%), added after World War I, lives in the east.[27]

> "This line drawn in the Fifth Century has undergone little change in the course of ages ... the separation between Walloons and Flemings has remained more or less apparent down to the present."
> Leon Van Der Essen, *A Short History of Belgium* (2012)

<u>Devolution of Competencies</u>. Like Switzerland, Belgium also supports ethnolinguistic governance with devolution. The devolution was from a

---

[25] This was actually the second vote for secession. A earlier vote for secession, in 2017, was declared invalid.

[26] German influence is increasing, as Italian speakers migrate to Ticino.

[27] German speakers do not have the right to use German in dealing with the Belgian government.

unitary federal system to linguistically segregated "Region" governments (territorial) and "Community" (cultural) governments. Devolution began in 1921 and occurred in six phases. Devolution was completed in 2011 and is so extreme that the jurisdiction of the Region and Community governments extends to foreign relations and international treaties that are within the scope of their extensive competencies. Thus, depending on the configuration of the Council of the EU (ministers), representation from Belgium can include multiple Region and Community officials, rather than having a single representative from the federal government. No other EU member does this.

However, unlike Switzerland, Belgium has a bilingual capital region and 27 municipalities with large linguistic minorities where linguistic congruence by segregation is not possible. In these mixed constituencies, consociational limits on majority rule and the use of the personality principle are both employed in an attempt to sufficiently reduce friction so that ethnolinguistic *detente* is possible. However, it is these partial departures from linguistic congruence that make governance in Belgium expensive, inefficient, and linguistically factional.

Cohabitation Strategies. Belgium facilitates the political cohabitation of its French-speaking and Dutch (Flemish)-speaking citizens, both federally and in the bilingual Brussels Capital Region (BCR), in two ways: (1) anti-majoritarian (consociational) rules and procedures and (2) use of the "personality principle."

Examples of anti-majoritarian rules and procedures include the following.

(1) Ministers in the federal government are *evenly* divided between French and Dutch speakers, even though 60% of Belgians speak Dutch. Decisions are made by cabinet consensus, which causes long delays and gives a veto to the minority.

(2) Belgium's federal parliament is divided into two language groups, French and Dutch, with requirements of a dual quorum and a dual majority vote on sensitive legislation. In addition, an "alarm bell" procedure

allows a super majority of either the French or Dutch parliamentarians, even though it is a minority of the Parliament, to defer an issue to the evenly divided executive branch in an attempt to negotiate a compromise.

(3) In the BCR, the Dutch-speaking minority is protected with anti-majoritarian requirements similar to those used at the federal level, although they are less than 10% of the BCR population. In addition to anti-majoritarian procedures, the personality principle is also recognized. French and Dutch (Flemish) have equal status in the BCR. Streets even have two names: one Dutch and the other French.

Language "Facilities" in 27 Municipal Governments. Other exceptions to Belgium's historic segregation are 27 border and rim municipalities. There are six rim municipalities on the periphery of the BCR and 21 border municipalities along the primary linguistic borders. In these constituencies, a limited form of the personality principle is used in an attempt to mitigate conflict.

The personality principle is incompletely expressed in the provision of government "facilities" for speakers of the second most common language.[28] Education in the second language is provided through the elementary grades, but not at the secondary level. As a result of the consequent perception of second-class status, the rim and border municipalities are a reservoir of friction from which conflict between French and Dutch speakers periodically emerges to divide all of Belgium along its linguistic seams.

"Every kingdom divided against itself will be ruined."
The Bible, Matthew 12:25

Dysfunction from Incomplete Congruence. Belgium's undemocratic and absurdly complex governance is a result of its lack of complete congruence. It is Europe's most dysfunctional nation-state. Ethnolinguistic division immobilized Belgium's federal government for approximately two

---

[28] Some of the BCR rim municipalities, which are in Dutch-speaking Flanders, have become majority Francophone. Their governments remain Dutch speaking, with facilities for the French speaking majority.

of the five years between 2007 and 2011. In 2010–11, Belgium had no functioning federal government for a year and a half—a world record for failure to form a new government after an election.

Ten months after Belgium's 2019 federal elections, a caretaker federal government was formed on an emergency basis for six months. This was compelled by the need to respond to the COVID-19 crisis. When the sixth month ended, in September 2020, the caretaker government of Prime Minister Sophie Wilmès was extended for an additional month as part of the 12th attempt to form a governing coalition. Thankfully, it succeeded. Ironically, the new prime minister is Alexander De Croo. He precipitated the 2010 crisis by withdrawing the Liberal Party's support for Prime Minister Yves Leterme.[29]

> "Far from being a model to reproduce, the Belgian example is pertinent in the sole measure that it is used to prevent similar developments in other federations."
>
> C. Van Wynsberghe, *The Belgian "Example", Weakness of the Federal Formula as Implemented in Belgium*

In summary, to approximate congruence Belgium has a complex system with linguistically divided Community and Region governments, an anorexic federal government, a *de jure* bilingual BCR, and 27 contentious municipalities with linguistic facilities. Only the inability to agree on the fate of the anomalous BCR, an overwhelmingly Francophone enclave inside of Dutch-speaking Flanders, prevents Belgium from dividing into two monolingual countries. Belgium's problematic lack of complete congruence is perhaps the best evidence for the importance of congruence.[30]

---

[29] The government collapsed after a seven-year-long dispute, from 2003 to 2010, over the boundaries of an election arrondissement (BHV) that combined the bilingual BCR and parts of Flemish Brabant (Halle and Vilvoorde).

[30] For a more complete discussion of language politics in Belgium: R. Blair, *Language Peace: The Seventh State Reform* (2019).

3.4 Bilingual Congruence in Post Colonial Nation-States

Complementary bilingualism is a neologism, but the phenomenon has roots in post-colonial language rationalization. The new governments in the former colonies needed a language of governance. There were many indigenous ethnolinguistic groups, so choosing any indigenous language would privilege its native speakers and outrage speakers of all other indigenous languages. Thus, choosing any indigenous language for congruence was rarely possible.

3.4.1 Indigenous Complementary Bilingualism. There were two former colonies that had an indigenous trade language not associated with one ethnolinguistic community. In choosing an indigenous trade language for governance, both governments set the stage for either monolingual congruence or complementary bilingualism. In both cases, the ultimate result remains undetermined. A desire to also learn a large international language has created tension between the proponents of combining an exogenous international language, such as English, with a single indigenous language and those who prioritize preserving more indigenous languages. Trilingualism is not feasible due to a lack of resources for the education system.

"The true creator is necessity, who is the mother of all invention."
Plato, *The Republic* (c. 375 BC)

Indonesia: Bahasa Indonesia Congruence. Indonesia's national motto is: "*Bhinneka Tunggal Ika.*" It means: "different, but the same kind." The phrase comes from a 14th Century poem celebrating tolerance between Buddhists and Muslims. Perhaps this helps to explain why Indonesia was able to appreciate the value of bilingual congruence.

With thousands of islands, hundreds of languages, and many ethnic, racial, and religious communities, Indonesia is exceptionally diverse in both geography and demography. To overcome these obstacles to unity, newly independent Indonesia used a very powerful tool—a common language. It needed linguistic congruence without the monolingualism of the European nation-state model.

In his 2019 book *Upheaval: Turning Points for Nations in Crisis,* Pulitzer Prize winner Jared Diamond wrote:

> "Today, I share with Indonesians their appreciation for the advantages of the wonderful Bahasa Indonesia as their national language. It's easy to learn. Only 18 years after Indonesia took over Dutch New Guinea and introduced Bahasa there, I found it being spoken even by uneducated New Guineans in remote villages."

"Bahasa" means language and "Bahasa Indonesia" means the language of Indonesia. Riau Malay, a regional trade language, was chosen to be the Bahasa Indonesia of the newly independent country. It was the first language of only 10% of Indonesia's population. As with all trade languages, Riau Malay had lost much of the unnecessary complexity, irregularity, and adornment that otherwise become attached to all natural languages. This made Bahasa Indonesia easier to learn, which is a crucial advantage.

In terms of implementing the decision to adopt Bahasa Indonesia, the government faced additional obstacles: (1) low literacy levels; (2) poor schools, if any, in many areas; (3) poor infrastructure for transportation and communication; and (4) little common history except for Dutch colonialism and Japanese occupation.

Bahasa Indonesia overcame all these obstacles. The superordinate goal of learning a unifying language created solidarity and demonstrated the cohesive effect of becoming a unified linguistic community. Bahasa Indonesia allows Indonesians to travel anywhere in their country and communicate as fellow citizens.

> "Tanzania is often castigated for the failure of its socialist experiment, but it is seldom given credit for success in national integration on the mainland. KiSwahili is part and parcel of that integrative triumph."
> Ali A. Mazrai and Alamin M. Mazrai, *The Power of Babel: Language and Governance in the African Experience* (1998)

Tanzania: KiSwahili Congruence. Indonesia is not the only former colony that achieved post-colonial linguistic congruence with an indigenous trade language. Tanzania did the same, using KiSwahili, where the prefix "Ki" is functionally equivalent to "Bahasa." Like Riau Malay, KiSwahili was the first language of only approximately 10% of the population. Tanzania's population of 35 million uses 125 languages. KiSwahili is particularly important in the fast-growing cities, where the speakers of other indigenous languages use it to unite socially and economically.

Indonesia and Tanzania: Diglossia or Complementary Bilingualism? Did Indonesia and Tanzania choose complementary bilingualism, or are they on a path to state-first monolingualism? When France mandated universal education in standard French, it created a hierarchical relationship between standard French and all of the other indigenous languages. This relationship is referred to as diglossia. In cases of diglossia, over time, there is a shift to a more prestigious language and a decline in the less prestigious languages. Are diglossia and language shifts occurring in Indonesia and Tanzania? If so, they have not established complementary bilingualism.

Indonesia. The 700+ languages of Indonesia (*bahasa nusantara*) include 13 languages that have at least a million speakers. These 13 languages are used by 70% of the total population. Many of the remaining languages are endangered, including approximately 450 with fewer than 1,000 speakers. Before 1953, local languages could be used as the language of instruction in elementary schools. This was a *de facto* policy of complementary bilingualism, with Bahasa Indonesia regarded as the unifying language (*bahasa persatuan*). From 1953 to 1975, the use of local languages was restricted to the first three years of schooling. This could be seen as a rebalancing of complementary bilingualism to accelerate the learning of Bahasa Indonesia.

However, in 1975 Bahasa Indonesia became the language of instruction at all levels. Recently, after an increase in local autonomy, the teaching of some local languages has been included in the curriculum in some regions—but as a subject and not as a language of instruction. English is a mandatory part of the curriculum.[31] This puts indigenous complementary bilingualism in competition with an elite exogenous bilingualism, using the combination of Bahasa Indonesia and English.

Indonesian students are taught multiple languages, but very few indigenous languages are taught in the education system and only Bahasa Indonesia is used as a language of instruction. Not surprisingly there is a decline in the use of most indigenous languages, which sometimes correlates with an increased use of larger indigenous languages in communities where they are taught as mandatory subjects.

Does Indonesia have incomplete complementary bilingualism, with Bahasa Indonesia used as a *bahasa persatuan* and a few other indigenous languages being protected, or will the emerging diglossia continue, with Bahasa Indonesia and English privileged as the national and international languages and all other indigenous languages declining? Does the current policy reflect local preferences, which should be respected? Are the preferences different in the cities than in the rural areas? Should Indonesia have an explicit national policy of 2MT complementary bilingualism to protect more indigenous languages? If so, is trilingualism possible with a third (international) language? The answers to these questions can only emerge with time and the effects of changing government policies.

> "Instead of inculcating a sense of accomplishment and opening windows to education, English became a frustrating barrier to my students." (Arguing for the extension of Kiswahili to secondary school.)
>
> Deo Ngonyani, *The Failure of Language Policy in Tanzania Schools* (1996)

Tanzania. In 1962, KiSwahili was adopted as the national language of Tanzania. In 1967, it was adopted as the language of governance. In 1968, it became the language of instruction in primary schools, with English being pragmatically retained for secondary education and university study. In 1984, KiSwahili was designated as the language of the social and political

---

[31] In religious schools, Arabic is often added.

sphere, as well as for adult education. In 2015, the Tanzania Ministry of Education and Vocational Training announced that KiSwahili would replace English in the secondary schools for the mandatory levels (1-4).

While primary education and the secondary schools' mandatory forms are taught in KiSwahili, the secondary schools' competitive levels, forms 5–6, are taught in English. Passing Form 6 is mandatory for continuing to university-level study, so English proficiency is a prerequisite (elite bilingualism) for post-secondary education. Except for KiSwahili, indigenous languages are not languages of instruction.

A policy of 2MT complementary bilingualism requires the use of diverse indigenous languages in the areas where they are predominant, as languages of instruction in the elementary-level grades,[32] with KiSwahili as a primary school subject and the language of instruction in the secondary-level grades. English would be an elective foreign language. Given the strong support for English, especially in private schools, such a policy implies a trilingual education, which may be too expensive for Tanzania— at least for now.

In cities, a *shift* to KiSwahili is replacing diverse mother-tongue languages, and in rural areas, a language *drift* is being experienced. The ethnic languages are adopting loan words from KiSwahili and experiencing "*KiSwahilzation*" of their grammar and pronunciation. In short, there is both language shift, primarily in cities, and language drift, primarily in rural areas.

The unanswered question is whether choosing KiSwahili as the sole language of instruction is a *de facto* policy of state-first monolingualism. Can and should Tanzania revert to a policy of 2MT complementary bilingualism? The answer depends on the availability of faculty and resources for the school system. As in Indonesia, the other former colony with an

---

[32] Such a policy should have the additional benefit of increasing the pool of potential elementary school teachers, making teacher training less arduous for future teachers and less expensive for the community.

indigenous common language, a choice appears to be emerging between preserving maximum linguistic diversity, using 2MT complementary bilingualism, or adopting Kiswahili–English elite bilingualism. Many parents prefer the Kiswahili–English combination for securing their children's economic future. Others fear that English will remain an elite language that institutionalizes elite closure, while a shift to KiSwahili eliminates other indigenous languages.

3.4.2 <u>Exogenous Complementary Bilingualism</u>. Most former colonies did not have a convenient trade language, like Riau Malay or KiSwahili. Choosing any indigenous language was impossible because privileging one language community disadvantages and alienates the others. In these cases, as determined by their new governments, the least divisive option was to continue using the former colonial language of administration as the new language of governance.

There were other significant benefits to using the colonial language: it provided efficient access to colonial records, avoided the need to translate them into multiple languages, and provided membership in a global linguistic network. However, as the colonial European language had been used for administration but not for governance, most of the population had little or no facility with it.

<u>Elite Bilingualism</u>. Use of the former colonial language was a marker of elite status. This resulted in elite bilingualism and elite closure. Because money for education was usually in short supply, wider dissemination of the elite language was slow. However, with sufficient resources allocated and an explicit policy of 2MT complementary bilingualism, elite bilingualism can be remedied. Indigenous languages will be used as languages of instruction, in the elementary schools of the communities where they are predominant. In establishing a policy of exogenous 2MT complementary bilingualism, it should always be kept in mind that elite bilingualism is a potential problem.

Retaining the colonial language as the national language avoided conflict between indigenous languages. This is the exogenous language advantage. With an exogenous common language, all indigenous languages are equal and 2MT bilingual congruence combines all of the indigenous languages with one exogenous international language.[33] A universally exogenous choice is the key to creating a global community of communication.

---

[33] Not necessarily a former colonial language. See Chapter 6.

"Our study has found that [bilingualism] can have demonstrable benefits, not only in language but in arithmetic, problem solving and enabling children to think creatively."

Dr. F. Lauchlan, School of Psychological Sciences and Health,
University of Strathclyde, Scotland (August 3, 2012).[34]

Chapter 4

Complementary Bilingualism: Congruence + Diversity

The preceding chapter explained *monolingual* congruence in the European nation-states and congruence in post-colonial nation-states. This chapter discusses the utility of *bilingual* congruence for the *multi-state* model (EU and AU) and for *multi-national* India. Complementary bilingualism is the only language rationalization policy that can, in each case, both establish congruence and preserve linguistic and cultural diversity.

"In 3 eye-tracking studies we show that 7-month-old infants, raised with 2 languages from birth, display improved cognitive control abilities compared with matched monolinguals."

Agnes Kovacs and Jacques Mehler, *Cognitive Gain in
7-month-old Bilingual Infants*, Proceedings of the National
Academy of Sciences, 106 (16) (April 21, 2009)

---

[34] F. Lauchlan, M. Parisi and R. Fadda. *Bilingualism in Sardinia and Scotland: Exploring the cognitive benefits of speaking a 'minority' language.* International Journal of Bilingualism (2012).

4.1 Bilingualism's Cognitive Benefits for Individuals

Before discussing language rationalization, this section discusses the benefits of bilingualism for individuals. An appreciation of these benefits will motivate greater support for 2 MT complementary bilingualism. The benefits include both individual cognitive benefits (4.1) and the maximization of the human potential of members of all language communities while preserving languages and cultural diversity (4.2).[35]

(1) <u>Lifelong Cognitive Benefits</u>. The cognitive benefits of bilingualism are found in babies, the elderly, and everyone in between. A study at the International School for Advanced Studies in Trieste, Italy, found that seven-month-old babies from bilingual homes were better at anticipating change, as measured by a faster switching of their anticipatory focus. At the other end of the age spectrum, a study of elderly bilinguals by the University of California (San Diego) found that bilingualism delayed the onset of cognitive decline and Alzheimer's. These benefits have also been documented in India.[36]

Cognitive reserve is increased by bilingualism as effectively as by increased education.[37] The better the second language skill, the greater the delay in the onset of symptoms and the longer the lifespan. By delaying the onset of decline, the mortality associated with dementia is reduced. Consequently, both quality of life and length of life are improved.

(2) <u>A More Nuanced Understanding of Words</u>. Children learning two languages follow the same pathway (milestones) at the same rate as those restricted to a monolingual education. However, studies suggest

---

[35] E. Bialystok, et al, *Bilingual Minds*, in Psychological Science in the Public Interest 10(2) (2009) and *Bilingualism: Consequences for Mind and Brain* in Trends in Cognitive Sciences 10(4) (2013).

[36] S. Alladi, et al., *Bilingualism Delays Age of Onset of Dementia, Independent of Education and Immigrant Status*, in Neurology 81(22) (2013).

[37] *Degree of bilingualism predicts age of diagnosis of Alzheimer's disease in low-education but not in highly educated Hispanics.* Neuropsychologia, Volume 49, Issue 14, December 2011.

that exposure to two lexical inventories gives bilingual children a better appreciation for the nuances of word meanings in both languages.

(3) Enhanced Dual Processing and Inhibition of Distraction. Bilinguals appear to be better at focusing (inhibition of distraction), switching between tasks (dual processing), and retaining information while performing tasks (dual processing). These are gains in executive control. Bilingualism trains the brain to perform better because bilinguals practice executive control when using two languages.

(4) Greater Creativity. If all of its other benefits are not enough, the interplay between two languages appears to induce greater creativity and enhance problem-solving.

This does not mean that bilingualism is a shortcut to producing superstar students. The scope and degree of the benefits need further study.[38] The point is that parents should demand an early and effective bilingual education for their children because (1) it may improve their children's academic and cognitive performance, (2) second-language acquisition is more successful when started early, and (3) the benefits of bilingualism will continue throughout the child's life. Bilingualism is not just for school-age children. Adults will also benefit.[39] People of all ages should study and practice a second language. It is never too late to start or to refresh an earlier bilingual capacity. Fluency is not necessary for benefits to accrue.

4.2 Maximizing Human Potential While Preserving Diversity

Parents who prioritize their children learning an international language need 2MT complementary bilingualism. Parents who prioritize their children's linguistic and cultural heritage also need 2MT complementary bilingualism. Citizens with common needs and interests, if they

---

[38] Correlation is suggestive of causation but does not prove it.

[39] T. H. Bak, et al., *Does Bilingualism Influence Cognitive* Aging, in Annals of Neurobiology 75 (6) (2014).

do not currently share a common language, need 2MT complementary bilingualism. Complementary bilingualism maximizes the potential of individuals from smaller language communities by adding a global language while preserving unlimited local diversity.

Maximizing Individual Potential. Ethnologue's 16th Edition lists 6,909 languages: 2,110 in Africa, 2,322 in Asia, 1,250 in the Pacific, 993 in the Western Hemisphere, and 234 in Europe.[40] Of these, approximately 500 are near extinction and a similar number are safe. That leaves almost 6,000 languages with fates yet to be determined. By removing much of the pressure for language shift, 2MT complementary bilingualism will allow more languages to survive and even flourish, sustaining greater cultural diversity.

The 10 most common languages (Mandarin, English, Hindi-Urdu, Spanish, Russian, Arabic, Bengali, Portuguese, Bahasa Indonesia, and French) are spoken by more than two and a half billion people. The top 20 languages account for more than half the world's population. The 500 "safe" languages are spoken by 90% of the world's population.

People who do not know one of the 500 safe languages are severely marginalized. These 750,000,000 people are often isolated from other language communities. Their languages often lack a standard dialect or written form. Not speaking one of the top 20 languages, a circumstance affecting 3,750,000,000 people, also limits their ability to fully benefit from the global exchange of information and ideas.

Please pause and reflect on these staggering statistics. Up to half of the world's population needs bilingualism to fully participate in the modern world while retaining their birth languages and associated cultures. This unfulfilled requirement is one of the largest human development issues of the 21st century and is being ignored. 2MT complementary

---

[40] The number of languages varies among sources, due to subjective distinctions between a language and a dialect.

bilingualism is the corresponding opportunity to increase human development and reduce both inequality and isolation.

Preserving Choice. What, if anything, should we do for the thousands of languages that are not safe? In dozens of books and hundreds of academic articles, linguists and other language mavens grapple with questions such as:

1) How many languages do we need? Does Papua New Guinea need over 800 languages? Does Europe need over 200 languages?

2) Which languages can be saved and which cannot? Is creating a written and oral record of a language enough, or must there be a population of speakers? If so, how many?

3) If there are multiple dialects with no consensus for selecting one as the standard, must we save every dialect? If not, how can we achieve sufficient agreement to produce a consensus dictionary and grammar? Who decides and what criteria should they use?

4) Can we put a value on a language? What does it cost to save a language? Who should pay? Who is willing to pay?

The answer to all these questions lies in preserving choice, which should be made as locally as possible. If people want to save a language, no other reason should be necessary. If they do not, no reason will be sufficient. The question is: "How can people exercise their language preference and still participate fully in the local, national, and international communities?" The only possibility that I know of is 2MT complementary bilingualism. Of course, linguists who are documenting endangered languages should continue to do so. My point is that 2 MT complementary bilingualism can help communities preserve their relatively small languages *in situ*, preserving not just the language but also the associated culture.

Increasing Access to Diversity. I know enough Spanish to read a newspaper and it is often interesting and enlightening to do so. Like most people, my curiosity exceeds my linguistic competence. One of the most appealing things to me about 2MT complementary bilingualism, as an individual, is its promise of access to new sources of information and viewpoints from cultures across the globe.

In a 1964 essay, *The African Writer and the English Language*, Chinua Achebe explained his decision to write in English: it was flexible enough for him to use English to express his African experience and gave him a much larger audience than any African language. He recalled reading Jorge Amodo's *Gabriella* in an English translation. It gave him a glimpse "of the exciting Afro-Latin culture, which is the pride of Brazil and is quite unlike any other culture." He noted that there were hundreds of other Brazilian writers, but "the vast majority will be closed to the rest of the world forever, including no doubt the work of some excellent writers." He concluded, "There is certainly a great advantage to writing in a world language." Anyone who has read Mr. Achebe in English is grateful for his linguistic dexterity.

Diglossia and Elite Bilingualism. The Anglophile position taken by Mr. Achebe has been criticized by some who wish to elevate the indigenous African languages and are concerned that elite bilingualism is detrimental to the prestige and development of indigenous languages. Neglect of indigenous languages can lead to diglossia and language shifts. Among these, the Kenyan writer Ngugi Wa Thiongo is one of the most outspoken.

> "...the bullet was the means of physical subjugation. Language was the means of spiritual subjugation."
>
> Ngugi Wa Thiongo, *Decolonizing the Mind: The Politics of Language in African Literature* (1986)

Mr. Achebe's response to Mr. Thiongo was to point out that his native Igbo language has six major dialects and its unification was the product of missionary interest in translating The Bible. Missionaries created Union Igbo by assembling six Christian converts, one from each dialect community, and combining the dialects "in a strange hodge-podge with no linguistic elegance, natural rhythm or oral authenticity." Mr. Achebe's disdain for what he sees as an exogenous (colonial) Union Igbo resonates to a degree with Mr. Thiongo's decolonizing position. Although Mr. Achebe's work has been translated into at least 30 languages, it has not been translated into Union Igbo. In contrast, Mr. Thiongo, writes in his native Gikuyu language but has been translated into English, in some cases by Mr. Thiongo.

Unquestionably, 2 MT complementary bilingualism can increase the audience for writers from smaller language communities. This would benefit both the writers and their expanded audiences. Small language communities would have access to global discourse, and other language communities would gain access to their ideas. At the same time, language shift and drift would be minimized by 2MT complementary bilingualism.

4.3 2MT (Mother Tongue) Complementary Bilingualism

The author's introduction to the concept of complementary bilingualism was through both his family and a result of growing up in Hawaii. It is worth a quick look to help the reader appreciate that 2MT complementary bilingualism is, in fact, a natural phenomena.

4.3.1 2MT Bilingualism. One of my brothers moved to Japan to teach English. He married a Japanese woman and they have two children. The children grew up speaking English with their father and Japanese with their mother. They attended primary schools in both Japan and Hawaii. The son attended high school at a boarding school in Indiana and took college courses in Hawaii, before graduating from Sophia University in Tokyo. The daughter studied English Literature at Doshisha University in Kyoto. She works as a translator. Both are comfortable in either a Japanese- or an English-speaking community. Transitioning easily between two very different languages and cultures, they are examples of identity bilingualism at the individual level. There is a crucial difference between my niece and nephew's identity bilingualism and someone learning a foreign language. Learning a foreign language builds a *lingua franca* communication bridge, but the learner is not a member of two communities.

4.3.2 Community Bilingualism. Before long-distance airline service, pineapple and sugarcane plantations were the foundation of Hawaii's economy. Plantations sourced their labor from several different countries and housed workers in ethnically segregated camps, in an ultimately unsuccessful effort to inhibit collective labor action. The primary labor sources were China, Japan, Portugal, Puerto Rico and the Philippines. The inevitable interaction of these language communities, with each other and with both English speakers and Hawaiian speakers, created a new pidgin that was built onto an older English-Hawaiian pidgin. When the new pidgin was used by plantation-born children as their primary language, it developed into a creole. Though still called "Pidgin," it is a complete language that linguists call Hawaii English Creole (HEC). HEC, because of its identity function, persisted even with the decline and demise of the plantation economy.

Plantation field workers had limited contact with native English speakers, but tourism changed that. With millions of English-speaking tourists from Canada and the mainland United States arriving every year, as well as thousands of in-migrants from the other 49 states, the plantation creole could easily have been overwhelmed. HEC avoided linguistic death precisely because it expressed a "local" identity in a language that could not be fully acquired, even after a long residence, unless exposure began as a child.

Hawaii's state government does not support HEC. The Department of Education is hostile, in the belief that any use of HEC at school undermines the student's acquisition of standard English. Although discouraged in the classroom, HEC rules the hallways and lunchroom. Beyond school, it has primacy in informal discourse among those born and raised in the islands. It is the language of courtship and gossip, to mention just two of its identity-affirming domains.

The "local" population, born in the islands, is 2MT bilingual in English and HEC.[41] English and HEC each encode an identity, like the identity bilingualism of my brother's children. Standard English encodes a national

---

[41] In rural and low-income communities, standard English is used less often and less completely. In higher-income areas, there is a degree of decreolization, in which standard English has diluted aspects of HEC.

(USA) identity and is used in formal domains. HEC encodes a local (Hawaii) identity. There is also the indigenous Hawaiian language. Hawaiians[42] are the quintessential locals, and Hawaiians who know their indigenous language along with HEC and English are examples of identity trilingualism.[43]

> "In fact, every political order conceived as a lasting institutional arrangement aspires to evoke and nurture the belief in its legitimacy."
> Christina von Haldenwang, *Measuring Legitimacy –*
> *New Trends, Old Short Comings* (2016)

4.4 The Utility of Congruence for Governance

Legitimacy is crucial because it greatly reduces the costs of governance. The greater a government's legitimacy, the more readily its citizens comply with its laws and policies. In contrast, governance without adequate legitimacy can be despotic or chaotic.

Linguistic congruence increases three crucial types of legitimacy: process legitimacy (democracy), outcome legitimacy (growth), and affective legitimacy (identity). For a multi-state and inchoate region-state (AU, EU) to successfully aggregate its nation-states, it must have congruence that is comparable to that of its member nation-states. Otherwise, nationalism will frustrate regionalism. Congruence is equally necessary for multi-national India's inchoate empire-state.

> "Democracy is inextricably bound with language and one wonders how it can be managed without a community of communication. Achieving meaningful, plurilingual democracy is a challenge that has not yet been taken up. It is perhaps the greatest obstacle to overcoming the EU's democratic deficit."
> Susan Wright, *Community and Communication: The Role of*
> *Language in Nation State Building and European Integration* (2000)

---

[42] "Hawaiian" refers to ethnicity; it is not a citizenship designation like the word "Californian."

[43] The author has two nephews who fit this description.

4.4.1 <u>Process Legitimacy: Democracy</u>. Region-states must be democratic because the 21st-century aggregation of nation-states must be consensual. Coercion is neither desirable nor possible. A regional democracy requires regional congruence.

Successful democracy is much more than the holding of free and fair elections. Elections are merely a tool with which a democracy periodically expresses an opinion about the job performance of incumbents and the relative appeal of challengers. Between elections, congruence permits the continuous dialogue which is a prerequisite for meaningful elections.

"Among people without fellow-feeling, especially if they read and speak different languages, the united public opinion necessary to the working of representative government cannot exist.... The same books, newspapers, pamphlets, speeches, do not reach them. One section does not know what opinions, or what instigations, are circulating in another."

John Stuart Mill, *Considerations on Representative Government* (1861)

Consider the definition of democracy in Abraham Lincoln's Gettysburg Address: "government of the people, by the people, for the people." Without linguistic congruence, there is not "the (one) people." Majority rule only makes sense if it is the majority of a community that recognizes itself as "us." This requires congruence between the institutions of governance and citizens. When elections are held, being outvoted by "others" is experienced as tyranny rather than democracy. A common language is necessary to avoid the feeling that you are governed by others.

"Democratic participation cannot be effectively institutionalized if people cannot talk to each other, nor can opportunities be equalized among citizens from all linguistic groups or feelings of solidarity develop, across ethnic boundaries."

Philippe Van Parjis, *The Linguistic Territorial Principle* (2011)

With region-state congruence, political parties can compete regionally in a single language that encodes the regional identity. Media can address all citizens with a single message, promote broader conversations, and document a common narrative. Candidates for regional office, such as for the presidency of the EU Commission,[44] can debate and campaign in a pan-European language. A directly elected Commission president who can speak to all Europeans in their common language would legitimize the EU in a powerful manner. The same is true for any other regional government.

"The relationship between linguistic variables and economic variables is the focus of a growing body of academic literature[45] on multilingualism."
European Parliament, European Strategy for Multilingualism: Benefits and Costs (2016)

4.4.2 <u>Outcome Legitimacy: Growth</u>. While no government can fully determine the performance of its economy, an improving economy increases the legitimacy of any government and economic failure decreases legitimacy. As legitimacy makes governance easier, a growing economy is important for successful governance. Europe's goal of economic integration includes four freedoms of movement: capitol, labor, services and goods. Congruence increases all four. It is particularly crucial for increasing freedom of movement for labor and services.

<u>Increased Trade</u>. With 2MT complementary bilingualism, the inchoate region-states and India will increase their internal trade. This captures the benefits on both sides of the trade. It is not controversial to state that a common language substantially increases trade. In February 2009, the European Economic Review published a study by Jan and Janko Fidrmuc

---

[44] The *Spitzenkandidaten* model, promoted by the EU Parliament, was not used to select the current head of the Commission. It is likely to return in some form. With congruence, the Commission president could be selected through a popular vote of all Europeans.

[45] M. Gazzola, F. Grin and B. A. Wickstrom (2015). "A concise bibliography of language economics," in *The Economics of Language Policy*, pp. 53-72, MIT Press, Cambridge, MA.

that looked at the economic influence of a common language (English) on EU trade.[46] They reached the following conclusions:

1) Gains from any *lingua franca*, in this case English, are equal to those from a common currency.

2) The availability of a *lingua franca* increases EU trade by 30% and is a main driver of international trade in Western Europe.

3) If EU countries increased their *lingua franca* proficiency by 10%, trade among them would increase by 14%.

4) If the other EU countries matched the success of the Netherlands in learning the *lingua franca*, it would increase their EU trade by 70%.

5) In the newer EU member states and candidate countries, the influence of a *lingua franca* is even greater. Trade is 74% higher than it would be without the current capacity in a *lingua franca*.

These *lingua franca* based benefits, substantial even under the EU policy of *laissez-faire* plurilingualism, will be magnified by 2MT complementary bilingualism. An easily learned and universally exogenous language, as discussed in Chapter 6, will best promote both internal and global trade.

"... for the single market to be effective, the Union needs a more mobile workforce."

European Commission, *A New Strategic Framework for Multilingualism* (2005)

Increased Labor and Service Mobility. The EU has done better in achieving two of the four freedoms of movement: free movement of

---

[46] See also: J. Melitz. *Language and foreign trade*, European Economic Review 52(4), (2008). J. Fidrmuc and J. Fidrmuc. *Foreign Languages and Trade*, Discussion Paper No. 7228 C.E.P.R London. (2009) "The language effect in international trade: A meta-analysis," *Economic Letters*, 116, (2012). P.H. Egger and F. Toubal "Common spoken language and international trade," in V. Ginsburgh and S. Weber (eds.), *The Palgrave Handbook of Economics and Language*, (2016).

capital and goods. It can do much better on the freedom of movement of labor and services. Labor and services can only move freely if the EU adopts 2MT complementary bilingualism. Increased competition among service providers and a greater ability of labor to migrate from high-unemployment areas to low-unemployment areas can increase competitiveness relative to the USA, China, and Russia—which have no barriers to those same four freedoms. The same would be true for the other inchoate region-state (AU) and for India.

4.4.3 <u>Affective Legitimacy: Identity</u>. Linguistic congruence, comparable to that of the nation-states and empire-states, is necessary to achieve comparable affective legitimacy. The process of establishing 2MT complementary bilingualism will be a superordinate goal that increases affective legitimacy *from the moment the policy is announced*. It is not necessary to fully achieve congruence for the positive effects to emerge. Working toward a common goal immediately strengthens a common identity and increases mutual trust. An *immediate effect is crucial* because the inchoate region-states and India need unity now, but 2MT complementary bilingualism may take a generation to complete!

The immediate effect of a common goal is best appreciated with an example of how working to achieve superordinate goals increases cohesion and cooperation. A University of Oklahoma study on group formation and intergroup dynamics recruited 22 boys to spend three weeks at a summer camp. Behind the facade of a summer's idyll, an experiment in social anthropology was conducted (Sherif, Muzafer, *Experiments in Group Conflict*. Scientific American vol. 195, 1956).

The boys were split into two groups and arrived at the camp separately. Initially, they were kept apart and unaware of each other. In the first week, each group engaged in activities designed to foster group identity and cohesion. Each group lived in a single dormitory, chose a group name (Eagles and Rattlers) and designed a shirt that displayed the group's name. Late in the first week, the groups were moved close enough to hear each other but not interact. Mere knowledge of another group's proximity created feelings of territoriality. Each group spontaneously expressed negative feelings about the unseen others.

In the second week, the groups participated in intergroup competitions. As expected, the competitions increased each group's solidarity as well as antipathy toward the other group. By the end of the second week the boys sometimes engaged in aggressive behaviors that required staff intervention. Hostility can be easily promoted using competition between groups with distinct identities.

In the final week, the two groups were combined and situations were contrived, such that to achieve mutually desired results the boys had to work together or compromise. By the end of the final week, the original groups had lost most of their salience and a general camaraderie emerged. Working together to achieve common goals replaced hostility with cooperation and solidarity.

A superordinate goal that produces direct communication where it was previously missing will be especially effective. An explicit goal of 2MT complementary bilingualism will help regions achieve many goals, including the fundamental goal of creating the strong identity necessary for political union. Congruence is the key to the creation of region-states.

Part III

Global Collective Action

"A reconstruction of the international system is the ultimate challenge....
The contemporary quest for world order will require a coherent strategy
to establish a concept of order within the various regions, and to relate
these regional orders to one another."

Henry Kissinger, *World Order* (2015)

Chapter 5

An Equitable Distribution of International Agency

This chapter and the final chapter discuss the ultimate topics of more
equitably sharing international agency and increasing our capacity for global
collective action. They are inseparable. So long as international agency is not
widely shared, the world order will not be conducive to equitable collective action. The empire-states that monopolize agency will be selfish and the smaller
polities that lack agency will, understandably, be both suspicious and resentful.

This chapter looks at increasing the international agency of India,
the EU and the AU. Its message, however, is equally applicable to both
the Community of Latin American and Caribbean States and to the
Association of South East Asian Nations, despite the fact that they have
not yet made an equivalent effort at regional integration. It may even
prove useful to overcoming the centrifugal forces in Dar al Islam.

"There is one angle of the world language question that has seldom if
ever been mentioned. It is the use of the world language for the solution of the internal problems in countries having large and numerous
linguistic minorities, or in which many languages are at present official."

Mario Pei, *One Language for the World* (1958)

5.1 Multi-National India's Bilingual Future

India is a multi-national empire without linguistic congruence. Unlike the three empire-states, post colonial India was unable to establish monolingual linguistic congruence. Its best option, at this point, is to establish congruence with 2MT complementary bilingualism.

"The Conference of Parties meeting in Paris in 2015 showed an Indian evolution to a new stance ... an India actively shaping the global agenda emerged."

A. Ayers, *Our Time Has Come: How India is Making Its Place in the World* (2018)

India: Make India Great Again. While India is not an empire-state, it has the potential to become one. India intends to take its place alongside the other three. Like China, India can look back to a golden age in its quest to recover its historic greatness and international agency. India's goal is to Make India Great Again. This will require linguistic congruence, perhaps with Hindi-Urdu or an exogenous language like English. Chapter 6 suggests a better option.

India has approximately 1800 indigenous languages. Hindi is the largest language, for 40% it is their native language. Bengali is second, but with only one-fifth as many native speakers. India has 29 languages with over a million native speakers. This contrasts dramatically with the linguistic situation in the three empire-states. In China, Putonghua is the language of congruence. Russian is similarly hegemonic in Russia, as is English in the USA.

Monolingual Congruence Fails. At India's formation, Article 343 of the 1948 Constitution stated that the Union would adopt Hindi as its language of congruence in 1965, using the Devanagari script. In 1963, the looming prospect of Hindi hegemony moved language policy to the top of the political agenda. As India's federal government prepared for the transition, non-Hindi speakers objected to Hindi hegemony. An ambiguous compromise was reached, according to which English "may" be used for official purposes after 1965.

The ambiguity was resolved differently in the minds of the Hindi-speaking plurality and the non-Hindi-speaking majority. Hindi's proponents interpreted the word "may" as providing the government with the authority to retain English but not as a requirement. The non-Hindi-speaking majority interpreted the word "may" as establishing a legal right to use English.

As the 1965 deadline approached, rioting broke out over the ambiguity and the deadline was deferred. In 1967, a new compromise gave English potential permanence by providing that it would retain its role as an alternative to Hindi, unless and until the legislative branches in each state where Hindi was not the official language endorsed the end of the English option.

As English is only spoken fluently by an elite minority, support for the English alternative to Hindi was not an endorsement of English as much as it was an expression of fear of linguistic hegemony by an indigenous language and the consequent privileging of its native-speakers. In some cases, especially in Tamil Nadu and other Dravidian-speaking areas in the South, linguistic concerns were combined with resistance to a centralized government based in the North. In other cases the language issue was a proxy for religious concerns. For example, Muslims wanted to preserve both Urdu and the Arabic script, despite the overwhelming similarity of Hindi and Urdu as spoken. Similarly, the Sikh religious community was concerned about the risk of language shift and wanted to protect the Punjabi language and Gurmukhi script.

On May 23, 2019, a landslide election victory gave Prime Minister Narendra Modi and the Bhartiya Janata Party (BJP) a mandate. As a result, Prime Minister Modi has the political capital necessary to change the course of India's history and, in doing so, accelerate its transition to an empire-state. Modi can use his mandate for a "Nixon goes to China" style breakthrough. President Nixon's consistent record of being strongly anti-communist enabled him, without domestic consequences, to make his historic trip to Beijing in 1972. Similarly, a popular Hindutvavadi prime minister may uniquely be able to resolve India's language rationalization stalemate without Hindi hegemony. The solution for Indian congruence is neither Hindi nor English. The best solution is 2MT complementary bilingualism with an exogenous and easily learned language. This will be discussed in Chapter 6.

> "The nation-state alone does not have a future."
>
> German Chancellor Angela Merkel (May 18, 2020)

5.2 Multi-State Europe's Bilingual Future

The aggregation of nation-states into region-states can balance the current dominance of the three empire-states and diffuse international agency more widely. This requires reproducing, at the regional level, the primary requirement for international agency: a polity capable of engaging in the "high politics" of security and international relations. The most advanced efforts, the EU and AU, have only made tentative efforts at establishing regional high politics. Until these regions become region-states with congruence, they will not be able to compete with the empire-states and, due to excessive nationalism, will remain vulnerable to "divide-and-conquer" strategies that reduce their agency.

Unity _and_ Diversity > Unity _in_ Diversity. The motto of the EU is "unity _in_ diversity." When an organization chooses an oxymoron for its motto, you can be sure it will excel at avoidance. Diversity, which has much to recommend it in other contexts, will never be the glue for unity. Europe needs unity _and_ diversity. It needs 2MT complementary bilingualism.

> "... to circumvent conflicts, European institutions have thus far avoided openly addressing the language question."
>
> Peter A. Kraus, _A Union of Diversity: Language,_
> _Identity and Polity Building in Europe_ (2008)

The language policies of the EU are divided between its institutional policy and its community policy. Complementary bilingualism will both unify and greatly improve both policies.

5.2.1 The EU Institutional Language Policy. The EU asserts that all 24 of its official languages are equal in the EU institutions. In the real world, achieving equality for all 24 official languages is a chimera. In practice, English is the first among equals. It is followed by French and German. Second and third places are converging and losing ground to elite English bilingualism. Nevertheless, Germans demand equality with French and French seek equality with English. The other member states cannot have equality.

The charade of equality reflects the EU's language policy paralysis. All of the language communities, even the three privileged ones, would be better served by a single and exogenous language that both minimizes and equalizes the linguistic burden of achieving congruence. That is only possible with an exogenous language and a policy of 2MT complementary bilingualism.

"A model using more than one common language, such as English, French and German, can simply not guarantee communication between all EU citizens, as they must inevitably have one language in common."

A. Bastardas-Boada, *Language and identity policies in the global age* (2012)

5.2.2 The Community Language Policy. The Treaty on the European Union (1992) granted the EU a new competence in the field of language education. A full decade later, the EU Council finally used this authority, but only in a very limited manner. It established an *aspirational* goal of mother tongue + two foreign languages (MT + 2). This is elite plurilingualism.

"44. The European Council calls for further action in this field [education] ... by teaching at least two foreign languages from a very early age...."

Barcelona European Council 15-16
March 2002 Presidency Conclusions

It left the implementation of the aspirational goal to the member states, who responded by maintaining their long-standing and failed policy of elite plurilingualism. This shifts the decision to individuals in a *de facto* policy that privileges English, Spanish, French and German, as these are the only options provided to most students. The choices of Europe's upper secondary (ICSD level 3) students in 2018, according to Eurostat, were: English 96.1%, Spanish 25.9%, French 22.0%, German 20.4%, Italian 3.1% and Russian 2.7%.

> "Despite the massive investment in the teaching of English in the education system ... there is still no common language that is widely spoken at a good or proficient level by the vast majority of European citizens."
>
> European Parliament, *European Strategy for Multilingualism: Benefits and Costs* (2016)

Except for occasional surveys based on unreliable self-evaluations,[47] there is no quantified data to indicate whether the massive effort to teach English has resulted in a substantial capacity to use English, whether there are trends or whether and to what extent what was learned is retained after leaving school.

> "The vast majority of respondents declared themselves as having an elementary or intermediate level of language competence ... (for English) only 20% assess their level as 'very good.' The level of language proficiency is not expected to improve considerably in the near future."
>
> European Parliament, *European Strategy for Multilingualism: Benefits and Costs* (2016)

The closest that the EU has ever come to generating useful data was the *First European Survey on Language Competencies: Final Report* (2012). Despite the title, this report was not repeated in the following decade. There is no measure of progress – if any. Its limitations were so severe that it has apparently resulted in no substantive policy changes. This is

---

[47] Kruger, Justin and David Dunning. *"Unskilled and Unaware of it: How Difficulties in Recognizing One's Own Incompetence Lead to Inflated Self-Assessments."* Journal of Personality and Social Psychology, Dec. 1999.

surprising, since the one thing it did establish was a great disparity among jurisdictions in the results of their teaching of foreign languages.

The biggest defect was that it only tested students while they were learning the languages. Thus, there is no measure of retention. It was, in effect, a peak measurement. A test of any language policy must also measure its long-term effects – years after the end of formal education. Language attrition is not well studied, but it appears that attrition in the five years after formal education is quite large when the language is not used on a regular basis.[48] A study of former students, five years or more after the end of formal education, would be very useful. Nevertheless, the limited data is sobering.

"The reported results indicated an overall low level of competences in both first and second foreign languages tested."

The European Survey on Language Competences: School-internal and External Factors in Language Learning (2012)

Despite the willful blindness, it is widely recognized that MT +2 plurilingualism has failed. Not surprisingly then, it is not what Europeans want. They want 2MT complementary bilingualism.

"You have to use both languages all the time. You won't get the bilingual benefit from occasional use."

Ellen Bialystock interview: *The Biliingual Advantage* in the New York Times (May 30, 2011).

5.2.3 EU Citizens Want Complementary Bilingualism. The EU is ignoring the clearly expressed desires of its citizens for both a common language and equal dignity for all of the official languages of the member states. In 2012, the European Commission released Special Eurobarometer 386, "*Europeans and Their Languages.*" The reported results were:

---

[48] Annual Review of Applied Linguistics, Volume 15, March 1995, pp. 151 - 164.

(1) A large majority of Europeans (81%) think that all languages spoken within the EU should be treated equally. Governments, in other words, should not privilege any European language community. Neither French congruence nor German congruence is an option. After Brexit, English may roughly meet the EU citizens' neutrality preference,[49] but English has already been tried (*de facto* if not *de jure*) and has failed. The result is elite bilingualism and inequality.

(2) Approximately seven in 10 (69%) also think that Europeans should be able to speak a common language. Europeans' appreciate the importance of congruence and want to become a European community of communication.

These two preferences of Europeans can only be reconciled through 2MT complementary bilingualism, with an easily acquired common language that is not the official language of any member state. If English is used, the problem will be the low probability of acquisition, compounded by problems of retention and inter-generational transfer. It will be a perpetual task of Sisyphean proportions. Moreover, English has cultural and ideological baggage as the elite language of the Anglo Sphere and its neoliberal economic agenda. Chapter 6 will compare English with an alternative that minimizes both the cost and difficulty of acquisition, retention, and inter-generational transmission. There are other options, but the comparison is useful for understanding the importance of making a carefully considered choice.

> "The absence of (and fear for) public debate on the language issue, has led to an EU public language policy which presents, first of all, a huge gap between the *de jure* and *de facto* situation and lacks coherence and transparency. In particular, clear friction may be noticed between, on the one hand, the need to create restricted language regimes and, on the other, the formal principle of equality of languages."
>
> Stefaan van der Jeught, *EU Language Law* (2015)

---

[49] English is an official language in two of the smallest EU member states, Ireland and Malta.

Complementary Bilingualism (2MT). Only one change is required to go from the current EU community policy of MT + 2 plurilingualism to 2MT complementary bilingualism: make one of the +2 languages a second MT that provides congruence.[50] Switching from the three languages of MT +2 plurilingualism to the two languages of 2MT complementary bilingualism will free up substantial time for students to study another subject. As EU congruence is achieved with the second MT,[51] those who still wish to acquire a third language can choose a non-European language.

5.2.4 EU Region-State Democracy. It took decades of effort, usually bloodshed and always coercion to achieve the territorial monolingualism that provided the European nation-states with congruence. Despite the great cost, the payoff was also great. Congruence provided an essential condition for democracy. Europe's current dilemma is its inability to achieve comparable democratic legitimacy at the level of the EU. Until there is congruence between EU institutions of governance and a European community of communication, the democratic deficit will retard "ever closer union." Like Belgium, the EU will be at risk of splintering.

A European community of communication will permit political parties to organize and campaign across Europe, not just form into coalitions of nation-state parties whose real agenda is success in their nation-state elections. Lack of congruence distances the government from its citizens and it distances the citizens from each other.

To create a European community that can be governed democratically requires integration in three dimensions: economic, political and civic. The EU is struggling at the intersection of the economic and political dimensions and has barely made any progress in the civic dimension. Economic

---

[50] It would simultaneously upgrade the institutional policy from elite multilingualism to complementary bilingualism.

[51] Learning complementary bilingualism could begin before formal schooling, just like monolingualism does, once parents are bilingual in the common language. This forms the basis for the 2MT designation.

integration isn't easy, but it is the easiest of the three. It was only when the Eurozone was established, necessitating a significant increase in political integration, that serious problems emerged.

The Eurozone and the EU are struggling at the intersection of economics and politics because the common currency triggered a common monetary policy in an area that was not optimal. A monetary policy that is suited to one part of the Eurozone is problematic for others. Thus, the existence of the common monetary policy creates a need to institutionalize a transfer mechanism. A consciousness of "us" is needed in order to sustain support for a transfer mechanism of indefinite duration. A transfer mechanism divides the interests of creditor nation-states from those of the debtor nation-states (eg. Germany vs Greece) and can only be sustained if there is an *overriding* common identity. The European identity is not, currently, adequate to sustain an indefinite transfer mechanism. Only congruence between a demos (citizens) and polity (institutions of governance) will permit open ended transfers.

The USA is also a suboptimal common currency area. It maintains a uniform monetary policy without difficulty only because it has robust transfer mechanisms. The USA identity is stronger than the EU identity in large measure because it has a common language. The common identity allows the transfers to occur, within a collective "us," without creating conflict. Because of the common language and identity, people and businesses can, if they choose, easily move from a transferor state to a transferee state. They do not often do so, because the transferee state, almost by definition, has lesser economic opportunities. The EU lacks a common language and, thus, a collective "us" does not exist in Europe as it does in the USA.

The third stage, a civic union, is harder still. It is harder because it cannot be done through economic policies or legislation. Only the people themselves can forge a civic community. It is not driven by pocketbook calculations or by the counting of the contents of ballot boxes, it is driven by empathy and the erasure of the distinction between "them" and "us."

How easily a civic solidarity can unravel was demonstrated in the summer of 2011. A serious outbreak of food borne illness in Germany affected almost 4000 people and killed over 50. On May 26, 2011, Germany blamed Spanish cucumbers, excluded them from the German market and notified other EU countries. The next day, the European Commission repeated the charge and specified two Andalusian farms as the source. The farms were closed and the sale of all Spanish produce was adversely affected. The losses to Spanish agriculture amounted to around $200 million per week. The source of the infection was later determined to be in Lower Saxony, Germany. The inevitable result was hard feelings and charges of German condescension and bullying. Similar charges were made by Greeks, throughout the Euro Crisis.

Economics does not require a civil community or any community, although a community is a more efficient economic space. Democratic governance requires a community. The third stage of creating a civic community requires sustained and direct communication among all of the members of the community. For the multi-state EU, it requires congruence that does not sacrifice diversity. That is only possible with 2MT complementary bilingualism.

5.2.5 <u>EU Region-State High Politics</u>. In addition to linguistic congruence, Europeans have strongly and consistently favored a common EU defense policy. In 2016, Standard Eurobarometer 85, entitled Europeans' views on the priorities of the European Union, reported that three quarters (74%) of Europeans support a common defense and security policy. Only the free movement of Europeans, at 79%, had more support. Over the period from 2004 to 2016, support for a common security and defense policy has been stable between 71% and 78%. As support in the United Kingdom was only 58%, post-Brexit support will have increased. Germany France and Spain were all above 80%.

A combination of factors has created a sense of urgency for the EU to become more self-reliant and less dependent on NATO: 1) President Trump precipitously declared NATO obsolete and complained, with some justification, about insufficient European defense spending. This raised the possibility that the US would shift its defense spending to the Pacific region without adequate time for Europe to assume a much greater role in its own defense. 2) The USA continues to run massive deficits that will eventually require significant spending reduction, including a reduction in the spending to subsidizes Europe's defense. This is likely to occur without sufficient warning to Europe's defense community. 3) Political stalemate in Washington has eroded the leadership capacity of the USA and 4) In 2014, Russia occupied the Crimean peninsula and, as of this writing in early March of 2022, it has invaded Ukraine. It is explicitly demanding a relationship with the Ukraine in which Russia is its suzerain.[52]

The military value of linguistic congruence is starkly revealed by the disparity between Russian high-politics and Europe's lack of high-politics. The Russian economy of 1.7 trillion (dollar equivalence) is 2% of the global economy of 85 trillion (dollar equivalence.) Russia's economy is #11 in the world. Four European nation-states have larger economies than Russia (Germany, Great Britain, France and Italy.)

The population of Russia is only 145 million. The population of the EU is over 500 million. The GDP of the EU is 13.4 trillion, about eight times as great as Russia's. Germany alone has a GDP of 4.32 trillion (dollar denominated), which is more than double Russia's. The EU members spend 225 billion (dollar equivalent) for defense, three times as much as Russia's 70 billion (dollar equivalent). There is no rational reason for the EU to be intimidated by Russia, except that the EU's latent power is wasted as a result of its lack of unity. It is the height of folly for the EU to fail to establish self-reliance in security and foreign affairs.[53]

"Countries will have to earmark forces for joint action and train them together. They must be able to make hard decisions together – or suffer

---

[52] The initial European response to the February 2022 invasion of Ukraine was surprisingly robust. It remains to be seen if this unity will extend beyond the crisis.

[53] It was only with the Russian invasion of Ukraine in February of 2022 that Germany, in particular, and the EU, in general, showed a serious interest in establishing a European capacity for high politics.

the consequences. After a transition period, collective security must be truly collective."

Leslie H. Gelb, *Lest Foreign Wars Engulf Us* (1993)

Less NATO, More Europe. Russia sees the USA as the primary threat. Shifting from a USA centric NATO to an equally robust but European defense and security regime should make Russia feel more secure and allow for a new equilibrium at a lower expenditure level. Russia can reallocate resources to Asia, where China is a historic adversary. A Russia that is focused on creating conflict with the EU clearly lacks a basic appreciation for its own future interests. A rational foreign policy for Russia would be focused on "ever closer union" with Europe and less dependence on China.[54]

Deescalation between the EU and Russia would be especially effective if Europe's nuclear deterrence was controlled by the EU. The only nuclear weapons now controlled by any EU member are a small number of French weapons. If these French weapons are transferred to an EU command, along with a necessary supplement from a denuclearized NATO, direct EU negotiations with Russia could establish a more stable European balance. Russia would feel more secure because the EU weapons would not be under the control of a competitor empire-state. Multi-state (EU) control would effectively make it impossible for the EU to use its jointly managed nuclear weapons in a first strike. The logical consequences would be for both Russia and the USA to reorient their weapons systems to a more Asian and polar orientation, increasing the security of Europe. This is premised, of course, on Europe translating its latent capacity into an actual capacity for high politics.

In summary, by continuing to rely on NATO after the end of the Cold War, Europe prioritized the cost savings from over reliance on an ally. Will the USA really sacrifice its citizens *en masse* in a nuclear exchange with

---

[54] China, within a few decades, will inevitably (global warming) seek to reverse two mid-19th Century "unequal treaties" with Russia (*The Convention of Peking* and the *Treaty of Aigun*) which transferred large parts of Manchuria to Russia.

Russia in order to protect Europe allies which it perceives as shirking their defense responsibilities? It is unlikely. The only plausible reasons for continuing the less secure reliance on NATO is that the EU political class lacks the imagination, cohesion and willpower for "ever closer union" in security and defense policy – even though Europeans have said that they want it.

The Belgian Solution: Reciprocal Bilingualism. It is one thing to *want* a common security policy and another to *implement* it. A good place to start rationalizing EU defense and security policy would be by rationalizing language use in a joint EU military forces. An EU defense force, unlike the EU parliament, cannot use 24 languages. There is already a successful European bilingual model in the reciprocal bilingualism of the Belgian Army Armed Forces.

Belgium had problems, particularly during World War I, with primarily French speaking officers leading troops that primarily spoke Dutch. The bias towards promoting French speaking officers persisted, to some degree, until the 1970's. Today, at induction, the language preference of a soldier is presumed to match that of their community of origin, unless they otherwise specify. Basic training is in that language and soldiers serve in monolingual units. Orders and commands are given in the soldier's first language.

Non-commissioned and commissioned officers are required to be fluent in either French or Dutch and to have a working knowledge of the other. Fluency in both French and Dutch is required for Majors and above. The percentage of officers who are native speakers now matches the community, with 40% native French speakers and 60% native Dutch speakers. There are no provisions for the soldiers whose native language is German. 2MT complementary bilingualism would be even better than the Belgian solution of reciprocal bilingualism, because it would extend to all military personnel regardless of rank.

If the EU implemented 2MT complementary bilingualism to unify its citizens, it would necessarily also unify Europe's military. Alternatively, 2MT complementary bilingualism that begins in an EU military will facilitate its adoption in civil society.

"There is not much sense in building Africa in sovereign States, independent of each other for we know that it is from our union and from it alone, that we shall draw sufficient strength to assert ourselves in the world."

François Tombalbaye, former President of the Republic of Chad

5.3 Multi-State Africa's Bilingual Future

No region has a greater need for 2MT complementary bilingualism than Africa.[55] It is needed both for regional unity and for the preservation of Africa's tremendous ethnolinguistic diversity. It is also needed for maximizing the human capital of Africa's many smaller language communities, for reducing poverty, for regional democracy, for regional high politics and for creating more rational political boundaries. Regional democracy and high politics, discussed above for the EU, is equally applicable to the AU and will not be repeated. As with the EU, the question of which language is the best choice for Africa is reserved for the sixth and final chapter.

"By far the greatest wrong which the departing colonialist inflicted on us and which we now continue to inflict on ourselves in our present state of disunity, was to leave us divided into economically unviable states which bear no possibility of real development."

Dr. Kwame Nkrumah, *Neo-Colonialism: The Last Stage of Imperialism* (1965)

---

[55] Although specific global problems are not addressed in this essay, it is important to note that Africa contributed very little to global warming but is already suffering greatly from its effects. It is among the first regions to be significantly affected and the effects will be disproportionately severe in Africa. In addition, Africa has little capacity to adapt. Global collective action is as important, if not more important, for Africa as for any other region.

5.3.1 <u>Establishing Rational Boundaries</u>. Europeans spent hundreds of years in bloody conflict establishing their current nation-state boundaries.[56] Africa's post-colonial leaders avoided a similar prolonged and painful process by retaining their colonial boundaries after successfully exorcising the colonial regimes. As colonial boundaries were established for the convenience of colonial governance, any degree of *rationality*, from the perspective of the indigenous population was merely serendipitous. Unfortunately, such serendipity was rare.

<u>Nation-State Boundaries (The Gambia and Cameroon)</u>. The effect of diverse colonial languages in the creation of irrational boundaries is clearly captured in the histories of The Gambia[57] and Cameroon. To a greater or lesser extent this is the reality across post-colonial Africa.

<u>The Gambia</u>. The Gambia, a narrow Anglophone nation-state hugging the banks of its namesake river, is a bizarre Anglophone enclave within Francophone Senegal. The Gambia was a small part of the Mali Empire (1235 to 1670). Once the largest kingdom in West Africa, the Mali Empire's former territory is now divided among seven West African countries.

Portuguese slave traders set up shop at the mouth of the Gambia River, by which slaves were transported from the interior. After abolishing slavery, the British replaced the Portuguese. The British only controlled the Gambia River and approximately 16 km along each bank. Except for its short Atlantic coast, The Gambia is entirely enclosed by Francophone Senegal.

The Gambia became independent in 1965. five years after Senegal. In 1981 a leftist coup attempt led The Gambia's president to request military aid from Senegal. This led to a confederation, in 1982, called

---

[56] Given the current circumstances in the Balkans and Ukraine, the task of establishing stable European nation-state boundaries is still incomplete.

[57] Like The Bahamas, The Gambia uses a definite pronoun (The) in its name.

the Senagambia Confederation. The linguistically divided Confederation lasted only seven years.

Were it not for the slave trade and European colonialism, The Gambia would never have existed. It is now an anachronism that needs to consolidate into a larger polity in order to achieve an adequate scale for a modern economy. That consolidation could be Senegambia, again, or it could be a larger West African polity based on the historic Mali Empire and the current Economic Community of West African States (ECOWAS) discussed below.

> "... the state system that first grew out of European feudalism and now, in the post-colonial period, covers virtually the entire earth provides the framework in which ethnic conflict occurs. Control of the state, control of *a* state, and exemption from control by others are the main goals of ethnic conflict."
>
> D.L. Horowitz, *Ethnic Groups in Conflict* (2nd Ed. 2000)

Cameroon. The 25+ million citizens of Cameroon speak over 250 languages. Its official languages of administration are both French and English. Cameroon also recognizes six other languages: Fula, Ewondo, Igbo, Chadian Arabic, Camfranglais and Cameroonian Pidgin English.

Cameroon (*Kamerun*) was a German colony from 1884 until 1919. After World War I it was divided by the League of Nations into the British mandate *Cameroon* and a French mandate *Cameroun*. In 1946 these league mandates became UN trusteeships. French Cameroun gained independence in 1960 and British Cameroon gained independence the following year. The two former trusteeships joined to become the Federal Republic of Cameroon.

Cameroon became a one-party state in 1966. In 1972 its federal system was abolished and power centralized. Ten semiautonomous regions are administered by elected regional councils but these are led by presidential appointees. After economic crises in the 1980s, multiparty politics was restored in 1990. Multiparty politics led to the creation of language based parties and pressure for greater autonomy in the Anglophone areas – even for complete secession and the creation of an Anglophone nation-state called the Republic of Ambazonia.

Since 2016, Cameroon's Anglophones have actively resisted Francophone hegemony. The linguistic divide, as in India, is also a proxy for other cleavages (ethnic and religious). The primary political cleavage is between a largely Anglophone party, the Social Democratic Front, and a largely Francophone party, the Cameroon Peoples Democratic Movement. Congruence in French seems very unlikely. 2MT complementary bilingualism with an exogenous choice other than English or French could be the solution to Cameroon's linguistic divide.

Regional Economic Community (REC) Boundaries. Africa's search for more rational boundaries uses economic convergence as its primary mechanism. The AU delegated responsibility for economic convergence to seven Regional Economic Communities (REC).[58] They are, at least roughly, seven African polities modeled on the EU. Of the seven REC, the Economic Community of West African States (ECOWAS) is the most integrated.[59] It has 15 nation-state members, but they are divided linguistically between an overwhelmingly Francophone group of eight, called the West African Economic and Monetary Union (UEMOA), and an overwhelmingly Anglophone group of six, the West African Monetary Zone (WAMZ).[60] One member, Cabo Verde, belongs to neither subgroup.[61]

---

[58]   The REC are: Community of Sahel-Saharan States (CEN-SAD); Common Market for Eastern and Southern Africa (COMESA); East African Community (EA); Economic Community of Central African States (ECCAS); Economic Community of West African States (ECOWAS); Intergovernmental Authority on Development (IGAD); South African Development Community (SADC).

[59]   It hopes to become a common currency union by 2027. Thus, the earlier discussion about the Eurozone and the intersection of economic and political unity is equally applicable to this REC.

[60]   One member, Guinea-Bissau, is Lusophone (Portuguese).

[61]   Its official language is Portuguese. Its national language is Cape Verde Creole.

"Of the many factors decisively affecting the capacity of the new governments to mount social, political and economic structures that were essential to the building of self governing nations, language was probably the most complex.

Abdulaziz and Fox, *"Evaluation Report on Survey of Language Use and Language Teaching of East Africa"* (1978)

It is clear from the experience of both the nation-states and the seven REC that the lack of congruence is complicating the search for rational boundaries. As in the EU, 2MT complementary bilingualism can eliminate linguistic barriers. This will permit any combination of Africa's nation-states or REC to join together into more economically and politically successful polities.

5.3.2 Preserving Diversity, Adding Unity. Africa has over 2,000 indigenous languages. The AU has defined all languages of Africa as official. In 2001, the AU created the African Academy of Languages to harmonize all 2,000 languages and safeguard the endangered ones. Only 2MT complementary bilingualism is capable of achieving this goal.

The AU has six working languages: KiSwahili, English, French, Arabic, Spanish, and Portuguese. Some of its Regional Economic Communities (REC) designate several of these working languages as their official languages. For example, the Economic Community of West African States (ECOWAS) uses French, English and Portuguese. The Community of Sahel-Saharan States (CEN-SAD) uses the same three and adds Arabic. This contrasts with the Intergovernmental Authority on Development (IGA) which uses only English.

None of the five exogenous language communities will defer to any of the other four, so all five are effectively excluded from consideration as a language of pan-African linguistic congruence. KiSwahili is an indigenous trade language and would be suitable for Africa's internal congruence, but the experience in Tanzania strongly suggests that its limited international reach will make it an unattractive choice for 2MT complementary bilingualism. As discussed earlier in the cases of both Indonesia and Tanzania, the optimal choice in order to avoid having to choose between preserving diversity and achieving global reach would be the pairing of an exogenous language with potentially global reach with each indigenous language in areas where it was predominant.

While English can be characterized as a global trade language, it lacks the most beneficial aspect of a true trade language – the loss of unnecessary complexity and adornment. For the AU, there is a compelling reason to exclude English. It is an official language in twenty-four of Africa's fifty-five nation-states. Privileging Africa's Anglophones would be resisted by Francophones and Lusophones (Portuguese). It would, in fact, be resisted by all Africans other than Anglophones. (It would be resisted heroically by Africa's proud Francophones.) The same degree of resistance would arise if the choice were French, Spanish, Portuguese or Arabic. KiSwahili would be resisted by those who insisted on joining a global language network. None of the official languages of the AU would be acceptable, precisely because they are official languages – they are already widely but not universally used. Chapter 6 will discuss a choice for 2MT complementary bilingualism that will allow Africa to preserve its diversity and still integrate linguistically into a global community of communication.

Preservation Without Unity Is Dangerous. Maintaining diversity is not an unmitigated blessing. Diversity can be accompanied by xenophobia. The fear of foreigners and strangers too often accompanies a strong identity in a pluralistic environment. If the EU motto is changed to Unity *and* Diversity, perhaps the AU should consider Diversity and Unity, reflecting its greater diversity. In both cases, the sentiment is the same as Indonesia's *Bhinneka Tunggal Ika*.

As Africa establishes more rational boundaries for greater economic growth, a unifying *bahasa persatuan* will be an essential element. The choice for a global *bahasa persatuan* is the subject of the final chapter.

5.3.3 Maximizing Human Potential. I'd like to repeat, for emphasis, two paragraphs from section 4.2. The point made in these two paragraphs is critical for Africa and South East Asia. These are the two regions with the greatest linguistic and cultural diversity and are home to most of the languages that are not "safe" from the threat of extinction.

"People who do not know one of the 500 safe languages are severely marginalized. These 750,000,000 people are often isolated from other language communities. Their languages often lack a standard dialect or written form. Not speaking one of the top 20 languages, a circumstance affecting 3,750,000,000 people, also limits their ability to fully benefit from the global exchange of information and ideas.

Please pause and reflect on these staggering statistics. Up to half of the world's population needs bilingualism to fully participate in the modern world while retaining their birth languages and associated cultures. This unfulfilled requirement is one of the largest human development issues of the 21st century and is being ignored. 2MT complementary bilingualism is the corresponding opportunity to increase human development and reduce both inequality and isolation."

There is one aspects of maximizing human potential that deserves special attention, decreasing poverty in future generations. This requires increasing trade within Africa, increasing Africa's market size and increasing its domestic manufacturing capacity.

Poverty Reduction: Increasing Intra-Regional Trade. As discussed above, in Section 4.4.2, 2MT complementary bilingualism will increase the four freedoms of movement (capital, goods, services and labor) that are the heart of regional economic integration. Imagine trying to start a business in The Gambia. You are in a tiny Anglophone country, but the vast majority of the customers nearest to you are Francophones.

Trade volume among African nations represents approximately 10% of their total trade. In comparison, intra-European trade is approximately 60% of the total trade of the EU. Clearly there is much room for improvement. Unlike Europe, which uses elite English bilingualism to facilitate the regional movement of capital and goods, Africa has multiple *lingua franca*, based on the diversity of its pre-independence colonial administrations.

In *Language and Foreign Trade*, Jacques Melitz looked at literacy, linguistic diversity, the distinction between direct communication and translation, the role of a *lingua franca* and network externalities. He found that 1) a common language increases trade; 2) direct communication is three times as effective as translation; 3) if a market has language barriers, there will be increased exogenous trade; and 4) trade is lower between countries with high linguistic diversity. These findings, along with the earlier discussion in section 4.4.2, support a policy of 2MT complementary bilingualism to increase intra Africa trade and, thereby, capture the full value of trade.

<u>Poverty Reduction: Domestic Manufacturing</u>. I am not advocating (or opposing) a formal policy of import substitution. I am not an economist and take no position on economic controversies. I am simply referring to the fact that the consolidation of polities will create larger markets and these markets will justify the shifting of manufacturing capacity into these markets to avoid tariffs and transportation costs. China's rise was made possible, in large measure, because of the size of its market. The African market, if united by linguistic congruence similar to the unifying effect of Putonghua in China, will soon be the largest market in the world. It is projected that by 2100 Nigeria alone will have the second largest population in the world – more than China, but less than India.

If both parties to trade are members of the African Union, unfavorable terms of trade are avoided. Terms of trade refers to the ratio export prices to import prices. In other words, the amount of imported goods that can be purchased per unit of exported goods. This leads to an improvement in living standards in the community where the goods are imported under improved terms of trade.

"... a language is never an end in itself. It is a tool with which one expects to achieve definite aims."

André Martinet, French Linguist (1908 – 1999)

Chapter 6

Increasing Our Capacity to Solve Global Problems

This chapter addresses the ultimate questions: (1) who should choose the language used for the creation of a global community of communication and (2) should the choice be an existing and already powerful natural language, such as English, or a universally exogenous and schematic language, such as Esperanto.

"It is hardly possible to overrate the value ... of placing human beings in contact with persons dissimilar to themselves, and with modes of thought and action unlike those with which they are familiar."

John Stuart Mills, *Principles of Political Economy* (1866)

6.1 The UN Adds a Seventh Language

The purposes of the UN as set forth in Article 1 of its charter, are:

1. To maintain international peace and security....

2. To develop friendly relations among nations based on respect for the principle of equal rights and self-determination of peoples, and to take other appropriate measures to strengthen universal peace;

3. To achieve international co-operation in solving international problems of an economic, social, cultural, or humanitarian character, and in promoting and encouraging respect for human rights and for fundamental freedoms for all without distinction as to race, sex, language, or religion; and

4. To be a centre for harmonizing the actions of nations in the attainment of these common ends.

All four of these purposes will be greatly advanced by the establishment of a global community of communication. Thus, establishing global 2MT complementary bilingualism should be the top UN priority. The UN is the ideal organization to make the choice of which language is globally optimal, after which the nation-states, inchoate region-states, REC and India can concur for their own needs and purposes. The UN choice could be made by simply designating a seventh official language for this purpose.[62]

6.2 The False Promise of *Lingua Franca* English

English is now the most widely used *lingua franca*. That the language of an average sized country situated off of the West Coast of Europe became a global *lingua franca* is not due to any characteristics that make English particularly suited to the role. Rather, it is because the British successfully established settlement colonies that displaced the indigenous populations in the vast spaces of North America and Australia.[63]

Great Britain's settlement colonies in North America and Australia-New Zealand had both the geographic blessing of distance from Eurasia

---

[62] Of course, if the UN does not show adequate leadership, the EU, the AU or India can and should initiate the process. Time is of the essence.

[63] Canada, the USA, Australia and New Zealand have over 7 times the population of England and are over 200 times as large. Although much of Canada is too cold for development and much of Australia is too hot, their relatively empty expanses have natural resources.

and a common language. When Eurasia was decimated by two wars in the first half of the 20th century, economic and military leadership shifted to Britain's former settlement colonies. At the end of World War II, the USA produced half of the world's manufactured goods. Even with the inevitable decline in the percentage of the world's GDP produced by Anglophones, as Eurasia recovered from its 20th-century wars, there has been no decline in the use of English as a *lingua franca*. The development of the Internet and other improvements in communication and transportation technology increased the global utility of *lingua franca* English— but only for elite communication and an elite identity.

6.2.1 <u>The Allure of English</u>. The Anglophone network of elite *lingua franca* bilingualism is the language network with both the largest size (1.35 billion) and the greatest breadth (global dispersal). On this basis, many people assume that it is the inevitable choice for global congruence. This is simply wrong (Chapter 1, Myth #5). There are three reasons for the persistence of *lingua franca* English, but they will all transfer to any language chosen for 2MT complementary bilingualism.

<u>Network Externalities.</u> If having more users increases the utility of a network, people choose a larger network over a smaller one. People join Meta (Facebook) because there are already hundreds of millions of users. Positive network externalities create a "bandwagon" effect. English has very positive network externalities.

<u>Path Dependence</u>. Once a practice is established, it is easier to conform than to change the standard. A classic example is the QWERTY layout of the English language keyboard. The arrangement of keys looks oddly random, but the layout was actually designed to make it hard to type fast. At a time when manual typewriters were prone to physical jamming, speed was not an unmitigated virtue. Now, even though manual typewriters are obsolete and physical jamming is not a problem, the QWERTY keyboard is still the standard. After many millions of keyboard users internalized the QWERTY arrangement, the cost of retraining them was not justified by a small gain in typing speed.

Probability Sensitivity. People will not learn a language unless there is a reasonable probability that its subsequent use will justify the effort. Without such a probability, there is insufficient motivation to learn any language. Globally, people expect to be able to use English more frequently and more widely (intensive and extensive) than any other foreign language. So, probability sensitivity encourages learning English as a foreign language and using it as a *lingua franca*.

This sounds impressive, until you realize that all three of these advantages also applied to the Russian language in Eastern Europe. As earlier noted, the exogenous use of Russian dropped by half in just 30 years. If the UN, EU, AU or India initiated 2MT complementary bilingualism in any other language, English as a Second Language (ESL) could suffer the same or a greater reduction.[64] Over 85% of the world's population does not speak any English and less than 5% are native speakers of English. The global percentage of English speakers is decreasing due to the below average birth rate in Anglophone countries. A universally exogenous choice will quickly surpass English in popularity (network externality) and will reverse the English advantage in path dependence and probability sensitivity.

> "The choice of language and the use to which language is put are central to a people's definition of themselves in relation to their natural and social environment, indeed in relation to the entire universe."
>
> Ngugi wa Thiong'o, *Decolonizing the Mind:*
> *The Politics of Language in African Literature* (1986)

Choosing English will almost certainly produce global English elite bilingualism. The EU demonstrates this problem with its failed *de facto* policy of English-centric plurilingualism. Used in a policy of 2MT complementary bilingualism, English would do better than under the EU's *laissez-faire* plurilingualism. Better is not good enough—that sets the bar

---

[64] The reduction in Russian occurred in the absence of a language rationalization policy. English as a second language (ESL) or *lingua franca* could suffer an even more dramatic decline after the adoption of 2MT complementary bilingualism.

too low. There are several reasons to reject English as a global community's common language, even if it were plausible (it is not) to contemplate its use in 2MT complementary bilingualism.

6.2.2 The Fallacy of Composition. The fallacy of composition refers to an erroneous belief that each individual's selection from the available options (restricted plurilingualism) will collectively produce the optimal outcome. A good example of the fallacy of composition is the paradox of thrift, popularized by the economist John Maynard Keynes.

When insufficient demand causes a recession, individuals increase their savings rate to have a cushion against the possibility of a job loss. The aggregate effect of these additional savings is a reduction in spending that further reduces demand. This makes the recession worse. The paradox can be overcome by offsetting the extra individual saving with extra government (collective action) spending, which is countercyclical. It restores the total demand and rebalances the economy. This shows the capacity of government action to overcome the negative results, at the community level, of rational individual choices.

The fallacy of composition in global language rationalization results in the privileging of English and the failure to consider other options. The fallacy of English inevitability needs to be challenged, if we are to find the best choice for global congruence. English is unlikely to achieve global congruence. Individuals choosing English plurilingualism are choosing elite bilingualism. Replacing elite bilingualism with 2MT complementary bilingualism overcomes the fallacy of composition.

> "... the massive degree of complexity that a language winds up clotted with if left alone is hopelessly unnecessary."
> John McWhorter *What Language Is* (2011)

6.2.3 *Laissez* Fail: The Difficulty of English. English has a head start. This advantage, however, is more than offset by the difficulty of its acquisition, maintenance, and intergenerational transmission. To better understand the difficulty of learning English, let us look at a related pair of problems: unpredictable English phonemes (sounds) and graphemes (spelling). They are two sides of a coin. In an easily learned language, there would be a strong correspondence between phonemes and graphemes. Correspondence allows students to predict the sound of a word from its written form and to know the spelling of a word from its sound. English, in this respect, is much further from the ideal than most languages.

> "Most of the opposition to simplified spelling is due to the fact that having taken the time and toil to master our atrociously inconsistent spelling, people have a vague fear that if a phonetic system were adopted, children, the ignorant classes and persons of poor memories would be able to spell just as well as they without one quarter the trouble of learning. Not that they are conscious of this childish and unworthy attitude, for usually they are not, but the motive is operative none the less."
>
> Henry Hazlitt, *Thinking as a Science* (1916)

In English, for example, the same sound can be written in 11 different ways: he, see, sea, seize, Caesar, people, amoeba, key, silly, believe, or marine. If you know the spelling and want to express the sound, you have the reverse problem. One letter in English can represent multiple sounds. For example, the letter "a" has different sounds in these eight words: a, father, wanted, many, village, dame, and, or badly. Another phoneme appears in thirteen different ways: go, mauve, yeoman, sew, roam, foe, oh, brooch, shoulder, flow, bureau, borough, or owe.

It is not just a problem with vowels. Each letter "c" in the words "Pacific Ocean" is pronounced very differently. The sound s is the same in these seven spellings: mess, cell, piece, psychology, science, schism and isthmus. The same phoneme is expressed five different ways in church, cello, bitch, question, and adventure.

Bahasa Indonesia and KiSwahili are completely phonic. This makes them significantly easier to learn. English could be made phonic, but it would require that the current 26 letters be increased to between 40 and

44 letters or accented letters. That, of course, isn't going to happen to English or any other major language.[65]

As a result of this poor correspondence, English-speaking children spend a significant part of their elementary education just learning how to spell their native language. It also takes longer to teach reading. For nonnative learners, this is a nightmare. Speakers of languages outside of the Indo-European family have an especially difficult time learning English, unless they are raised in a bilingual (2MT) household, like my niece and nephew in Japan.

> "Unfortunately, even the most diligent students with the most responsible teachers often cannot communicate effectively with the target population after 10 years of studying English."
>
> Keith P. Campbell and Zhao Yong, *The Dilemma of English Language Instruction in the People's Republic of China*. TESOL Journal, v2 n4 p4-6 Summer 1993

Other serious problems with the English lexical inventory include its use of contronyms, where the same word is used for opposite meanings, homographs, where words with identical sound and/or spelling have different meanings and an excessive use of idioms. Plurals are usually formed by adding the letter s as in day-days, but not always: man-men, mouse-mice, child-children, deer-deer, tooth-teeth and army-armies are just some of the alternatives. All natural languages have idiosyncrasies. With English it is a matter of degree.

There Isn't an English Language. Because there is no academy to regulate the English language, there are many Englishes. As George Bernard Shaw is alleged to have quipped: "England and America are two nations divided by a common language." In addition to English, Canadian, Australian, New Zealandish, and Amglish (American English) there is

---

[65] Hawaiian uses only 13 phonemes, five vowels and eight consonants. Ta'a, formerly known as Southern Khoisan, has 130 consonants, 28 vowels and, as if that was not enough, three tones.

also Chinglish (Chinese English), Singlish (Singapore English), Hinglish (Hindi English) and scores of other markedly diverse macaronic and dialectic variations. The lack of a standard English assures that English will never be able to support a common identity and will be problematic for global communication. It can only produce an elite bilingualism that privileges Anglophones and neoliberal capitalism.

"Modern English grammar is, in a word, weird."

John McWhorter, *Our Magnificent Bastard Tongue:*
The Untold Story of English (2008)

Basic English. The problems for ESL students are so great and well known that the strongest advocates of English have tried to make it more accessible. In the first half of the 20th Century, two men clearly saw its difficulty as an impediment to a larger global role for English. One of them is well known: Prime Minister Winston Churchill. The second is less well known: Charles K. Ogden, the designer of Basic English.

In an attempt to replace elite bilingualism, Ogden designed Basic English as a minimal version of English. It had a vocabulary of only 850 words. Basic English was intended to be both a way to teach English and a candidate for the role of global language. As a potential global language, it received substantial attention near the end of the Second World War. Prime Minister Churchill established a cabinet level committee on Basic English. His committee recommended that Basic English be used by British diplomats and the British Broadcasting Corporation. Unfortunately for Basic English, Churchill's party lost control of Parliament in 1945 and the new Labor government abandoned his initiative.

Even if Basic English had received Labor support, it would have failed to become a global language. Severely restricting the vocabulary impairs expressive capacity. Basic English could adequately express mundane necessities, but lacked the ability to express complex ideas with precision or beauty. To my knowledge, no one has ever found a way to make learning English a less overwhelming task.

"Speaking English makes people open to Britain's cultural achievements, social values and business aims."

The British Council, *English 2000* (1995)

6.2.4 *Laissez* Unfair: The Caste System. It is a great advantage to be able to use your native language. It seems very unfair when someone else's language is used. One of the best expressions of this unfairness came from a Swiss psychologist who worked as a translator at the UN from 1956 to 1961 and later for the World Health Organization (WHO). He characterized the elite bilingualism of *lingua franca* English as a linguistic caste system.

"An English-speaking physicist has been able to devote to physics the many hours that his colleagues from other cultures have had to devote to the painful and slow acquisition of English, but he is unaware of his privilege. When you are a member of the upper caste, you take your advantages for granted... Not only have people outside the upper caste been forced to devote many, many hours to the study of the upper caste's language, moreover when they have to negotiate or discuss with somebody belonging to this upper caste they are at a disadvantage: their opponent can avail himself of a richness of vocabulary and a feeling of security in language use that they will forever be lacking. Their opponent has a mastery of the language weapon, they have not."[66]

Unwarranted privilege can be so subtle or indirect that people are unaware of it. For example, news that is delivered in a local language may well have been curated by a news agency that is owned and operated by Anglophones. This will be invisible to the ultimate consumers of the content. To overcome unwarranted privileges, government language rationalization should focus on finding an easily learned language that, because it is universally exogenous, does not favor any "upper caste."

---

[66] C. Piron, *Le défi des languages* (1994).

"Speaking English makes people open to Britain's cultural achievements, social values and business aims."

The British Council, *English 2000* (1995)

6.2.5 The Neoliberal Anglo Sphere. Privileging Anglophones is, to some degree, privileging neoliberal capitalism. Neoliberal capitalism has produced some of the most serious problems that global collective action needs to solve, such as global warming and the inequality that results from the un-disciplined drive to increase capital without limit or an ultimate purpose.[67] Capitalism can be successful for individuals and simultaneously fatal for communities, another example of the fallacy of composition. Can neoliberal capitalism's excesses be effectively constrained in a world where Anglophones are linguistically privileged? At a minimum, it will be more difficult.

Stopping Zombie Capitalism's Excesses. The greatest threat to our planet comes from the combination of zombie politics and zombie capitalism. Instead of seeing Adam Smith's invisible hand as a useful means of establishing prices and making market defined allocations, zombie economics engages in the mindless production of nonessential and disposable commodities for the sole purpose of an endless accumulation of capital. It is both irrational and immoral. It causes global warming and prevents an adequate response to global warming.

"Transnational corporations have become the dominant force directing our world. Humanity is accelerating towards a precipice of over con-sumption and the large transnational are the primary agents driving us there."

Jeremy Lent, *Five Ways to Curb the Power of Corporations*
(Open Democracy, July 22, 2018)

Nation-State Sovereignty is Useful to Zombie Capitalism. Nation-states lack the ability to harmonize their policies. Zero-sum competition

---

[67] Goethe's poem, *The Sorcerer's Apprentice*, or the Disney version in the movie *Fantasia* comes to mind. It is a good metaphor for hubris and uncontrolled recursive actions.

among nation-states allows transnational capital to avoid taxation and regulation. Global capital does not even need to collude. It is unified by its reflexive support for externalizing costs onto society, tax avoidance and reduced government oversight and regulation. Capital easily outmaneuvers the individual nation-states at the expense of global equity and our planet's future.

If you list countries and corporations together, ranked according to revenue, 71 of the top 100 are corporations. Only 29 are countries. Each of the top six corporations has annual revenues in excess of the annual tax collection of India.

Twenty of the top 100 (listed below) are almost exclusively dependent on the production or burning of fossil fuels. Their collective influence makes it much harder for governments to respond appropriately to global warming. The total annual revenues of just these twenty is over 3.8 trillion dollars, more than the annual revenue of the USA government. This list only includes the very largest of those businesses which are dependent on generating atmospheric pollution. A comprehensive list, including both smaller and more diversified corporations, would yield a far larger total figure.

13. State Grid (China)	38. Daimler	80. BMW
16. China National Petroleum	43. General Motors	82. Nissan
18. Royal Dutch Shell	47. Saudi Aramco	83. China Railway
20. Exxon Mobil	49. Total	86. Gazprom
21. Volkswagen	56. Chevron	88. Petrobras
22. Toyota	57. E.ON (Germany)	97. ENI (Italy)
24. British Petroleum	63. Honda	

While governments try to limit the influence of other governments, they are shockingly open to being influenced by global capital. Fewer and larger polities could more easily agree and coordinate their policies for the global taxation and regulation of international capital. Region-states are one way to improve this coordination. Global governance is a better response. Effective global governance could equitably tax and regulate international corporations, so global capital prefers nation-states that lack agency and inchoate region-states with a severely limited political capacity.

I am an Anglophone, but I believe that English should not be chosen unless and until it has been deemed acceptable by most non-Anglophones—that is equally true for any of the three empire-states' languages or even the language of a large nation-state. In addition to considering neutrality, the selection must also consider how easily learned the choice will be, relative to the alternatives, in order to avoid elite closure.

"We seem to have a collective blind spot when it comes to language design. We designed a better horse, it is called a car. We designed a better ox, it is called a tractor. Why do so many people think that only "natural" languages work properly?"

Russell Blair, *Making Europeans and Governing Diversity* (2016)

6.3 A Universally Exogenous and Schematic Language Choice

For the greatest contrast with English, the best comparison is with Esperanto. Esperanto is the only designed language that has entered the world's collective consciousness. It was designed at the end of the 19th century by Lazarus L. Zamenhof, with the objective of creating an easily learned and culturally neutral language[68] that would promote harmony among people from different language communities. Why has it not been more successful?

"Why should language have forms that are just cussed exceptions to a rule? What are they good for, besides giving children a way to make cute

---

[68] It is actually Eurocentric. However, a design which attempted to blend elements all of the world's language families would be a horrific mess. The difference are too numerous and mutually incompatible for there to be an option that is equidistance from all language families. While it is Eurocentric, Esperanto is universally exogenous and that is the key requirement.

errors, providing material for humorous verse, and making life miserable for foreign language students?

Professor Steven Pinker *Words and Rules:*
The Ingredients of Language (1999)

6.3.1 It is Now Time for a Designed Language. Is there any other aspect of modern life which is immune to the application of logic and reason? If architecture was as hidebound, we would still be living in caves. So why have designed languages been so unsuccessful?

Timing is Critical. The timing of Esperanto's launch could not have been worse. Germany was established in 1871, and Italy was fully unified by the contemporaneous inclusion of Rome. Thus, when Esperanto was created in 1887, Europe was enchanted by a romantic idealization of the ethnolinguistic nation-state model: one people, one government, and one language. Nationalism was revolutionizing European politics and Esperanto was only embraced by the few with the exceptional prescience to foresee the need for an antidote to the divisiveness that was latent in the nation-state model and emerged, horrifically, in two world wars.

Times change. Our understanding and our needs are different in the 21st Century. Remarkably, Esperanto survived and is now more clearly needed than ever before. We need a global community to solve global problems. This is a new development in human history and, while we have yet to fully appreciate it, only the most obtuse can deny it.

"Without official recognition, the fate of the best system (of language rationalization) is precarious; with it, any scheme that is not totally unworkable would do well enough."

Albert Léon Guérard, *A Short History of the*
International Language Movement (1921)

Is Esperanto Right for the 21st century? Albert Guérard (quoted above for a second time) was right a century ago and his point is equally valid today. Without official recognition Esperanto is a dream. With official recognition it becomes brilliant! A schematic choice is easier to learn than any natural language. Esperanto is the only tested and reliable, off-the-shelf linguistic software that is schematic and therefore easy to learn.

Lack of Geographic Base. Another problem for designed languages is the lack of a geographic base. A designed language is detached from every community, so it lacks many of the benefits that motivate students. The choice of Esperanto, as part of a 2MT complementary bilingualism policy, however, will attach it to every region that adopts it for congruence. In short, all Esperanto's historic problems will disappear with a simple vote of the UN, EU, AU or India.

Remarkably, despite the unfortunate timing, lack of a geographic home, and lack of official recognition, Esperanto persevered for 130 years. It has been used for every conceivable linguistic task, from daily conversation to academic and technical writing. It is the only designed language that has been tested in the real world and that has shown itself to be fit for all purposes.

6.3.2 The Schematic (Design) Advantage. Schematic (rule based) languages are easier to learn than chaotic natural languages. Governments that appreciate both the need to make the task of learning as easy and inexpensive as possible and the need for a universally exogenous choice will choose a schematic (designed) language. Once the UN, the EU, the AU or India chooses a language for linguistic congruence, hundreds of millions of people across the globe will immediately begin learning that language.

Lexical Growth. Loan words from many language families have already found their way into Esperanto. Like any language, Esperanto permits lexical growth. It has been growing for 130 years and has the capacity to meet the changing and expanding needs of its users.

"Esperanto, as we know it today, is not the work of Zamenhof. It is a language which has developed on the foundation of Zamenhof's project through a century of constant use by a very diverse people."
Claude Piron. Psychological Aspects of the World Language Problem and of Esperanto. Talk given in Basil Switzerland on March 21, 1998

Esperanto may be especially good at borrowing roots from isolating languages like Putonghua.[69] Esperanto can attach its affixes to phonemes from any language (it cannot, however, use tones to distinguish lexical or grammatical differences, and the written form should use a single orthography).

Esperanto is completely regular in its phonetic structure—like the always regular Spanish vowels. This contrasts with English, which is phonically chaotic. This phonemic regularity means that it can represent and incorporate any word that uses or adapts to its phonic inventory. Roots acquired from any language would then be multiplied by Esperanto's extensive use of affixes, which is a fundamental schematic feature of Esperanto.

Acquisition, Maintenance, and Transmission. A global language policy must be based on cost-effective acquisition, maintenance, and intergenerational transmission. Otherwise, the EU failure with English may be repeated. All three aspects must be addressed, in order to avoid elite closure. Esperanto, in a global or regional language rationalization policy of 2MT complementary bilingualism meets all three requirements for success: (1) ease of acquisition, (2) regular use for maintenance, and (3) 2MT (intra family) transmission.

Acquisition: An Order of Magnitude Easier. Anyone who has ever studied a foreign language knows that learning a natural language is very difficult.[70] For elite bilingualism to be avoided, it is important to use an easily learned language. Thus, Zamenhof got it right on the most important characteristic: it must be easy to learn— even easier than the trade languages in Tanzania (KiSwahili) and Indonesia (Bahasa Indonesia).

Did Zamenhof succeed? The Institute of Cybernetic Pedagogy (Germany) compared Esperanto with three natural languages (English,

---

[69] Isolating languages have morpheme to word ratios close to one and little or no inflectional morphology. In many cases, each word is a single morpheme.

[70] For non-schematic languages, the estimates vary from 1500 to 10,000 h. The former is for functional literacy, whereas the latter is for equivalence to native speaker fluency.

German, and Italian) in terms of the study time required for French high-school students to obtain equivalent facility. It took approximately one-tenth as long for French high-school students to achieve an equivalent level of Esperanto (150 h) as English (1500 h).[71] Given the limited time available for classroom instruction in the school year, students will be much more successful at learning Esperanto than English.

> "An average college senior or graduate in 20 hours of study will be able to understand printed and spoken Esperanto better than he understands French or German or Italian or Spanish after a hundred hours of study."
> Edward L. Thorndike, *Institute of Educational Research Language Learning Report.* Columbia University Teachers College (1933)

The results for the Francophone students were very impressive. As both French and Italian are Romance languages, it took the French students less time to learn Italian than German. English, though a Germanic language, is heavily influenced by French and fell between German and Italian. The important figure is the huge difference between learning any of the natural languages and learning Esperanto.

German	2000 hours
English	1500 hours
Italian	1000 hours
Esperanto	150 hours

Globally, hundreds of millions of students study English. This represents a huge investment by governments and institutions, in addition to the students' massive investment of time and effort. The results are

---

[71] Esperanto cannot be learned in 150 hours, nor can English be learned in 1500. The significance is that an equivalent learning occurred in one-tenth of the time.

discouraging. Outside of Europe, less than 1% of the students become fluent in English.[72] This is neither the fault of the teachers nor their students. Why fail with English when you can succeed with Esperanto?

The Paderborn Method: A Free Language. In Cybernetics (the study of communication and control in both animals and machines) the word propaedeutic references an introductory experience. A schematic propaedeutic (introductory-reference) language increases the student's understanding of their native language, better than any other second language, and also sets the stage for the efficient learning of a third language. Most of the time spent learning a propaedeutic language is recovered by a reduction in the time and effort required for learning other languages. In that sense, it is a free language – trilingualism for the price of bilingualism and the easiest way to learn another MT.[73]

The introductory-reference value of Esperanto has been studied since 1918. Generally, these studies have not been rigorously controlled and are not widely reported, in part because it is expensive to use students in a multiyear study and there was insufficient funding. Bias may also be a factor in some of the studies. The results, therefore, are somewhat anecdotal. Still, the results are consistent in two respects: 1) Designed languages can be much easier to learn than natural languages, and 2) Learning a highly regular and easy language reduces the time required to subsequently learn a natural language. Logic and common sense support these two observations.

Studies of the Propaedeutic Value of a Schematic (Esperanto) Language

1. 1918-1921 Girls Middle School students in Bishop Auckland College, England Dr. Alexander Fischer, *Language By Way of Esperanto.*

---

[72] C. Piron. *Communication Linguistique Etude comparative faite sur le terrain*, Language Problems and Language Planning 26(1), (2002).

[73] This has never been tested. But, when 2MT bilinguals are formally taught grammar, it would be logical to teach the schematic grammar first.

2. 1922-1924 Bishop's Elementary School, Auckland, New Zealand.

3. 1924 Wellesley College, Psychology Department, Mass., USA. Christian Rudmick, *The Wellesley College Danish-Esperanto Experiment.*

4. 1925-31 Columbia University and IALA, New York, USA. Edward Thorndike, *Language Learning.* Bureau of Publications of Teachers College, 1933.

5. 1934-1935 Public High School students in New York, USA. Helen S. Eaton, *An Experiment in Language Learning.* Modern Language Journal Vol 19, No. 1 (October 1934).

6. 1947-1951 Grammar School students in Sheffield England. J. H. Halloran (lecturer in Pedagogy at the University of Sheffield), *A four year experiment in Esperanto as an introduction to French.* British Journal of Educational Psychology, vol.22, n.3, Nov. 1952.

7. 1948-1965 Egerton Park School, Manchester, England. Norman Williams, *Report on the Teaching of Esperanto From 1948 to 1965.*

8. 1958-1963 Somero Middle School, Finland by the Ministry of Public Instruction.

9. 1962-1963 Eötvös Lorand University, Budapest, Hungary.

10. 1971-1977 International League of Esperanto Teachers coordinated studies in Hungary, Belgium, France, Greece, West Germany and the Netherlands.

11. 1970-1980 Institute of Pedagogic Cybernetics, University of Paderborn, Germany Prof. Helmar Frank.

12. 1983-1988 Elementary Schools, esp. Rocca Elementary School, San Salvatore di Logorno, Genoa, Italy.

13. 1994-2000 Monash University, Victoria, Australia.[74]

---

[74] See also: Raif MARKARIAN, *The Educational Value of Esperanto Teaching in the Schools,* In: R. Schultz & V. Schultz (compilers) *The solution to our language problems.* (1964). and R. Selten: *The Costs of European Linguistic (non)Communication.* (1997).

In the 70's, the University of Paderboren, Germany, was the center of study into propaedeutic language learning. Professor Helmar Frank studied the introductory-reference value of Esperanto by teaching it to students before they studied English.

One group studied only English. A second group spent two years studying Esperanto and then started learning English. The English only group established a big lead during the first two years, because the other group only studied Esperanto. In years three and four, the Esperanto first students were catching up, but were still behind in learning English.

By the end of the 5th year, the Esperanto group had learned as much English in three years as the English only group learned in five years. After the sixth year, the Esperanto group tested higher in English skills – even though they had only four years of English study compared to the six years in the English only group. The reason for this unexpected result is that the learning of any language, especially a schematic language, makes it easier to learn other languages.

Two other significant benefits have been reported: 1) the lower meta-linguistic load of the propaedeutic language permits efficient learning at an earlier age, and 2) student's who perform poorly in learning a natural language achieve greater success by first learning a introductory – reference (propaedeutic) language. These are both important benefits.

> "Language maintenance has been very little researched so far, but deserves much more attention in future linguistic investigations, since it appears to be the most crucial aspect of the language acquisition process."
>
> Herdina and Jessner, *The Dynamics of Third Language Acquisition* (2000)

Maintenance. People are unlikely to migrate to a community that uses a language they do not understand, except under extreme pressure. Despite the proximity of multiple countries and the unifying elements of EU governance, such as the Euro Zone, Schengen area, and *aquis communitaire*,[75] only 2% of the EU's citizens live in a country other than their birth country. Consequently, after learning a foreign language, there is little opportunity to use it. The result is foreign language atrophy.

In contrast, 2MT complementary bilingualism will allow everyone to practice their common language every day, even if they never leave their birth country, as well as permit them to travel and work anywhere without encountering a linguistic barrier. Being part of a global community will be crucial for generations who must live with the consequences of the current failure to provide effective and equitable collective action to resolve global problems.

Intergenerational Transmission. Our first and best teachers are our parents. From the perspective of government budgets, they are certainly the most cost-effective. A policy of 2MT complementary bilingualism will benefit from this simple fact. Just as one of the author's brothers and his wife raised their two children as bilinguals and a sister-in-law had two sons who achieved identity trilingualism (4.3) a policy of 2MT bilingualism will allow parents who are 2MT bilinguals to raise their children as 2MT bilinguals, starting from birth.

In schools, both of the students MTs will be taught in the same manner—as both a subject and as a language of instruction. This will somewhat resemble the Luxembourg situation described earlier. It will, however, be more than 50% easier, because (1) a policy of 2MT will add only one, rather than two, languages, and (2) learning a schematic language is much easier than learning a second natural language.

6.3.3 A Design Showcase: Afrançais. It is important for the reader who wants to go deeper to see how powerful a schematic approach can be. For that purpose only, I've added a quick look at how three simple changes to French would make it much easier to learn.

---

[75] The cumulative legislation and court decisions regulating EU members.

This part is taken from the English translation of a 2012 essay entitled: *Afrançais: Le français en tant que langue africaine.*[76] To be clear, it is reproduced here only to show the power of a schematic design. Like Basic English, Afrançais would not be a universally exogenous choice and is, therefore, suboptimal.

A Designed Dialect of French

The Three Elements of Afrançais

Most of the first two years of learning French is spent learning (1) irregular verbs and (2) the complexities of verb conjugation. Removing the irregularities and simplifying conjugation makes learning the Afrançais dialect much easier. For people who know French, learning Afrançais takes very little time and effort. For people who don't, it takes far less time and effort than learning standard French.

Element 1. <u>Infinitive Roots = 100% Regular Verbs</u>. In Afrançais, all verbs are regular. The many irregular verbs in French are not consistently irregular, so students need to memorize: 1) which verbs are irregular, 2) in which tenses they are irregular and 3) their irregular forms. The irregular verbs are even more important and troublesome than their very substantial number suggests, because they include the most commonly used verbs.[77]

Afrançais makes all French verbs regular by using the infinitive form of the verb (the way words appear in a dictionary) as the root for its conjugation. Where the final letter of the infinitive is a vowel, it is dropped. This allows vowels to be used as the conjugation suffix

---

[76] Given the love of the French language by its speakers, this heresy may both show the power of a schematic choice and make any schematic alternative to Afrançais very attractive to Francophones..

[77] There is an excellent explanation for this general linguistic phenomenon in *Words and Rules* by Stephen Pinker.

without creating diphthongs (vowel pairs). Using the infinitive as the root makes it easy to recognize the meaning, both in written and oral use. Instant recognition is the key to conversational fluency and very helpful in reading.

The following box displays three of the most common French verbs, one from each of the three verb types (-er, -ir and -re), in the present indicative conjugation. After each verb, the invariant form in Afrançais is at the far right shown and underlined.

être – to be	je suis	tu es	il est	<u>êtro</u>
	nous sommes	vous êtes	ils sont	
avoir – to have	j'ai	tu as	il a	<u>avoiro</u>
	nous avons	vous avez	ils ont	
boire – to drink	je bois,	tu bois,	il boit	<u>boiro</u>
	nous buvons	vous buvez	ils boivent	

Element 2. <u>Five Endings = Easy Verb Conjugation</u>. The second and final step is to add one of five single vowel suffixes, to show the tense, aspect and mood (TAM) [78] of the verb. Verbs in French use 84 suffixes to show tense, aspect, mood, and person. Unlike standard French, Afrançais doesn't mark the verb to show "person." Since the subject pronoun is always used, marking verbs to reflect person is unnecessary.

Because the compound tenses use the same five vowel endings as their corresponding simple tense, applied to either *avoir* or *être*, plus the present participle, you just use the five endings of the simple tenses, plus the past participles. The five endings are: 1) adding the letter "o" forms the present tense in the indicative mood, 2) adding the letter "u" forms the present tense (subjunctive mood), 3) adding the letter "a" forms the past tense in

---

[78] Tense refers to time – past, present or future. Aspect refers to whether the verbs action or state is unitary (perfective), continuous or repeated (imperfective). Mood refers to the subjunctive, indicative, infinitive and conditional forms of the verb.

the indicative mood, 4) adding the letter "e" forms the future tense, 5) adding the letter "i" forms the conditional mood.[79]

Conjugation is simple, as shown in this chart:

simple tenses	Afrançais	compound tenses	Afrançais
present indicative	infinitive + o	passé compose	avoir + o + participle
present subjunctive	infinitive + u	perfect subjunctive	avoir + u + participle
imperfect indicative	infinitive + a	past perfect indicative	avoir + a + participle
future	infinitive + e	future perfect	avoir + e + participle
conditional	infinitive + i	conditional perfect	avoir + i + participle

Since the greatest challenge to language proficiency is conversation. It is a huge advantage to only need to recognize and produce a small fraction of what standard French requires.

The next chart shows the relative simplicity of verbs in the Afrançais dialect. These five endings (a, e, i o, u) represent an 88% reduction in the memorization that is required to learn the standard French conjugation – and this is *in addition to* the reduction in memorization due to the absence of irregular forms.

Comparing Afrançais with Standard French Verb Conjugation (Guarder)

[79] In Afrançais, the imperative mood is expressed with the bare infinitive. Tone and volume convey the degree of urgency. Standard French has four endings for the imperative mood. In effect, the imperative is a new use of the infinitive mood.

French Simple Tenses	Afrançais	French Compound Tenses	Afrançais
Present (Indicative) garde gardons gardes gardez garde gardent	garder<u>o</u>	**Passé Compose (Indicative)** ai gardé avons gardé as gardé avez gardé a gardé ont gardé	avoir<u>o</u> guarder
Imperfect (Indicative) gardais gardions gardais gardiez gardait gardaient	garder<u>a</u>	**Past Perfect (Indicative)** avais gardé avions gardé avais gardé aviez gardé avait gardé avaient gardé	avoir<u>a</u> guarder
Passé Simple gardai gardâmes gardas gardâtes garda gardèrent	omitted	**Passé Anterior** eus gardé eûmes gardé eus gardé eûtes gardé eut gardé eurent gardé	omitted
Future garderai garderons garderas garderez gardera garderont	garder<u>e</u>	**Future Perfect** aurai gardé aurons gardé auras gardé aurez gardé aura gardé auront gardé	avoir<u>e</u> guarder
Conditional garderais garderions garderais garderiez garderait garderaient	garder<u>i</u>	**Conditional Perfect** aurais gardé aurions gardé aurais gardé auriez gardé aurait gardé auraient gardé	avoir<u>i</u> guarder
Present (Subjunctive) garde gardions gardes gardiez garde gardent	garder<u>u</u>	**Perfect (Subjunctive)** aie gardé ayons gardé aies gardé ayez gardé ait gardé aient gardé	avoir<u>u</u> guarder
Imperfect (Subjunctive) gardasse gardassions gardasses gardassiez gardât gardassent	omitted	**Past Perfect (Subjunctive)** eusse gardé eussions gardé eusses gardé eussiez gardé eût gardé eussent gardé	omitted

Combining the 88% reduction in conjugation with not having to memorize the irregular verbs means that learning the Afrançais dialect requires a small fraction of the effort required for learning verbs in standard French. Instead of verbs taking up half of the textbook and most of the cognitive load on students, they will require only a few pages.

Element 3. <u>No Grammatical Gender</u>. The term "gender" in linguistics means "type, class, sort or kind." *Natural gender* marking is when a word changes to reflect a real biological distinction. For example, English reflects natural gender in the third person singular personal pronoun with "he" or "she." *Grammatical gender*, in contrast, is the completely pointless marking of non-biological classes and their adjectives. Learning grammatical gender creates two problems for students: 1) learning the gender for each noun and 2) remembering to show agreement between nouns and their adjectives. Grammatical gender in both the Germanic and Romance languages perpetuates the confusion of the two meanings of "gender" by referring to masculine and feminine genders even even though the classes do not have any biological meaning.[80]

<u>Nouns</u>. Most European languages – but not English, the Altaic, Austonesian, Sino-Tibetan, Uralic and Native American languages- have retained vestiges of anachronistic grammatical gender. It clearly isn't necessary. In the Romance languages, grammatical gender assigns nouns to either a masculine or feminine class. The Germanic languages, excluding English, include a third class, called "neuter." There's no logic reflected in these pseudo gender assignments. For example:

1. In Spanish, "bikini" is a masculine noun (el bikini).

2. "Nose" is masculine in Portuguese (o nariz), but feminine in Spanish (la nariz).

---

[80] Gender in many other languages has retained a grammatical function. For example, KiSwahili has over a dozen noun categories (genders) with grammatical functions. The prefix Ki, as an example, is a grammatical gender marking used to mark a language.

3. Silverware requires three genders in German: the knife (<u>das</u> messer), the fork (<u>der</u> gabel) and the spoon (<u>die</u> loffel)?

4. In French, the word for beard (la barbe) is feminine. A woman's breast is masculine (le sein), but a mans chest is feminine (la poitrine).

This list of illogical and arbitrary categorizations could go on for many pages. What does all this false gender represent? Nothing useful. They are artifacts from the distant past.[81]

<u>Pronouns, Articles and Adjectives</u>. In Afrançais, the shorter form, previously called the masculine, is used. Adjectives are never marked for gender.

	Standard French Dialect	Afrançais Dialect
third person subject **pronouns**	il, elle (natural gender) ils, elles	il, elle (natural gender) ils
definite articles	le, la	le
indefinite articles	un, une	un
adjectives	grand, grande	grand

End of Section 6.3.3: A Design Showcase: Afrançaise

6.3.4 <u>The Internet: Teacher Training and Autodidacts</u>. Because Esperanto is a very easy language, students and autodidacts can use the internet to learn Esperanto. There are already on-line courses available for learning Esperanto and they can easily scale up serve an unlimited number of students. New ones will proliferate after any 2 MT selection. [82]

<u>Autodidacts</u>. Completing an online course in Esperanto is the equivalent

---

[81]   There are a few words where gender still has a semantic function. For example: le vase (the vase) and la vase (the mud). These will need to be dealt with, along with other details, in corpus planning.

[82]   For example, Duolingo currently has 100 courses in 40 languages. It is free, with ads, and very affordable without ads. The Esperanto course currently serves thousands of learners.

of a European B-2 level or four semesters at a university in the USA.[83] It takes about half the time to complete the online course. There are millions of students currently learning a language online. If Esperanto is chosen for 2MT complementary bilingualism in any significant polity, other providers (Babbel, Rosetta Stone, etc.) will quickly supplement what is currently available. It will be a very competitive environment. The "free with ads" model and the economics of scale will make it readily available in countries without a strong second language program in their school system.

Teacher Retraining. Language teachers have both a knowledge of a specific language and the extensive training required of all language teachers. With an easily learned language, they can utilize their extensive teacher training after a short period of on-line learning of the highly schematic language. This would not be the case with a natural language. Teacher retraining is important and, for Esperanto, much easier than for any natural language.

"The best time to plant a tree was 20 years ago. The second best time is now."

African proverb

6.4 Complementary Bilingualism Changes Everything

The earlier discussion of *superordinate goals* (4.3.3) pointed out that "Working toward a common goal immediately strengthens a common identity and increases mutual trust. An *immediate effect is crucial* because the inchoate region-states and India need unity as soon as possible, but full rationalization may take a generation to complete!" The same immediate effect will allow us to become a global community as soon as we begin learning any selected language. A global community is essential if our children and grandchildren are to avoid the intergenerational genocide

---

[83] E. Tschirner, *Listening and Reading Proficiency Levels of College Students* (2016). F. Rubio and J.F. Hackey, *Proficiency vs Performance: What do the tests show?* (2019).

that is being driven by zombie capitalism in a world without an adequate capacity for global collective action.

> "The hallmark of wisdom is asking, What effects will the decision I make today have on future generations? On the health of the planet?"
>
> Jane Goodall, *Book of Hope: A Survival Guide for Trying Times* (2021)

The UN: Global Congruence. Any large polity that chooses to establish an explicit language rationalization policy of 2MT complementary bilingualism (UN, EU, AU, India, etc.) will generate a powerful "gravitational" effect. Because any reasonable choice is sufficient, others will gravitate to the first mover's choice. Ideally, but not inevitably, the global *bahasa persatuan* should be chosen by the UN.

By adding Esperanto as its seventh official language, the UN will be the first mover. Explicitly or implicitly, this endorses 2MT bilingualism for the creation of a global community of communication. The UN also announces that the seventh language will become its universal pivot language for translations and the seventh language texts will be the reference text for resolving ambiguities among translations. The EU, the AU and India will almost certainly follow suit. The UN's seventh language will, immediately, become the most important second language for students in all countries.

The Non-Anglophone Empire-States. China and Russia will adopt the UN choice for global language rationalization, in part to eliminate the English-speaking global caste system. While universal complementary bilingualism will ultimately dilute the empire-states' monopoly of international agency, there will be no way to resist the gravitational pull of a global community of communication.

The Nation-States: Preserving Diversity. To preserve their linguistic diversity and achieve linguistic congruence, many nation-states will establish 2MT complementary bilingualism with the seventh UN language as the common language. This will include both nation-states with internal language conflicts (Belgium, Cameroon, Nepal and Sri Lanka) and those with high linguistic diversity: Nigeria (517), Cameroon (250), Brazil (217), Democratic Republic of the Congo (212), The Philippines (183), Malaysia (133) and Chad (130). The nation-states representing all 3,750,000,000 people who do not speak one of the top 20 languages will adopt 2MT complementary bilingualism in order to address their human development goals through greater access to information and greater international opportunities for their citizens.

Anglophones. While the Anglophone polities may not be early adopters, individual Anglophones will see the benefits and learn Esperanto – replacing the currently most popular foreign language choices of French and Spanish. Anglophones are notoriously bad at learning a second language, largely due to the privileging of their mother tongue, but this will change as they will appreciate the value of joining a global community of communication. Students everywhere will appreciate the reduced cognitive burden of learning a schematic language instead of a natural language.

"... the adoption of an international language is the greatest gift with which we could collectively endow our children and their descendants. We need it now, but they will need it infinitely more than we do."

Mario Pei, *One Language for the World* (1958)

Do you feel like the prisoner of a *status quo* that is marching towards the apocalypse with the intelligence and foresight of a zombie? That is, unfortunately, a valid metaphor. Fortunately, however, you do not need to be a passive victim of this brain-dead, intergenerational genocide. The collective peril of Generations Todos Juntos (Generations All Together) is also the key to realizing collective agency. You can change the world - you must change the world - to protect your future and the future of humanity.

Generations Todos Juntos must become a community of communication. That is the essential first step in creating a common identity and global political movement. The existential crisis is a unique political opportunity. You can make history. You must make history.

For 130 years, Esperantists argued the value of a designed language in the context of foreign language acquisition. English prevailed and Esperanto barely survived. The terms of the contest, however, have now changed radically. Utility based on the communication function of a large *lingua franca*, or any random natural language that is taught as a second language, is rapidly decreasing as a result of the tremendous advances in machine translation technology (MTT). The low probability of success outside of Northern Europe and the awful cost/benefit ratio will, with little warning, make *lingua franca* English irrelevant.

At the same time as the communication function is taken over by MTT, the increasingly severe and, indeed, existential nature of our global problems make it necessary to establish a global community – starting with a global community of communication that uses a universal identity language. That is why we need 2MT complementary bilingualism and, for 2MT complementary bilingualism we need an *easily learned and universally exogenous* choice. We need a rationally designed language and Esperanto has, in surviving for well over a century, expanded into all linguistic domains and proven its capacity for use in the full range of our global language needs. For the third and final time, please consider this important point:

> "Without official recognition, the fate of the best system [of language rationalization] is precarious; with it, any scheme that is not totally unworkable would do well enough."
>
> Albert Léon Guérard, *A Short History of the International Language Movement* (1921)

Thank you for reading the essay. Now, please, take a picture of the cover and send it to your friends. Ask them to buy a copy of the ebook (99 cents). This will save trees and is the least expensive way to spread the message. (The author receives only the minimum royalty at this price.) The ideas expressed should not be monetized when the stakes are existential. It is your future - you must act!